A HEADTEACHER'S DIARY

MAKING IT UP AS WE GO ALONG

TRYING TO LEAD A SCHOOL THROUGH A PANDEMIC

BY ALAN GARNETT

Dedicated to
Ellie, Jack and Betsy
xxx

Published in Great Britain in 2021 by Independent Publishing Network
Copyright © 2021 North Primary School and Nursery
John Harper Street, Colchester, Essex, CO1 1RP
www.northschool.org.uk

ISBN: 978-1-80049-677-4
A catalogue record of this book is available from the British Library.
All profits from book sales go to North Primary School and Nursery.

Printed by TJ Books Ltd

Design by Laura Davison

Cover image by Ronald Suffield

Contents

North Primary School and Nursery

Foreword

by Sir Bob Russell

In 2020 the World faced a pandemic when a virus hitherto unknown - Coronavirus, titled Covid-19 - spread rapidly, with infections quickly running into millions. By March 2021 more than 50 million had been infected around the globe. In the United Kingdom, around 125,000 people lost their lives.

The virus originated in China at some point in December 2019 and took hold in the UK from March 2020.

From mid-March all schools in the UK were required to shut, other than for the children of key workers and children falling into the category of 'vulnerable'.

This was an experience never before witnessed in the 125 years history of North Primary School and Nursery. It is Colchester's oldest primary school, located in a high-density residential area mid-way in the mile between the main railway station and town centre.

For most pupils, home education was introduced with teachers providing lesson material electronically.

Headteacher Alan Garnett, in his 20th year as the School's head, kept a daily diary of this remarkable period in the life of the School – and this was published each week in the Colchester Daily Gazette.

His diary is now published in this book, a record of how one School continued to operate during unprecedented times. While no two schools will have had identical experiences, what Alan Garnett has written will resonate with all involved in the nation's education during that challenging year and the first months of 2021. It will be of interest not only to those who were directly involved in education, and others with an interest in this period of our nation's history, but also for social historians in the years to come.

Sir Bob Russell and Lady Russell have had an association with North School for 50 years. Their four children attended North, as did their two youngest grandchildren during the pandemic. Sir Bob is a former Mayor of Colchester and for 18 years was the town's Member of Parliament. He now holds the honorary title of High Steward of Colchester.

Preface

by Alan Garnett, Headteacher

Sir Bob Russell, a dear friend and great ambassador to North School, suggested I keep a diary of how the unfolding events of the pandemic were impacting on school life. He said it would be a fitting addition to the School archive as we were three months into a year of celebrations to commemorate our 125th Anniversary. His proposal included ghost written entries which covered the lead up to the 23rd March 2020.

And just over a year later I was writing my 44th weekly episode, all of which had been published in the Colchester Daily Gazette, albeit in edited form. And here they are, in full, in one place. A chronicle of how one school community reacted to unfolding events.

I have not edited the diary to appear clever after the event. The diary is honest in that respect. Sometimes I have surprised myself, appearing almost prescient, other times foolish - guilty of being a little precious or just plain wrong. You will come to your own conclusions. You will not have to wade through lots of footnotes. I have not tried to excuse or explain my errors.

The only editing I have done is to sift out repetitious labelling necessary to explain terms afresh to the Gazette's readership each week. I have included a glossary - all professions have their initials and acronyms.

Please do not come here looking for elegant prose. I am a headteacher not a writer. If the book has any merit, it is in the description of how one school reacted to the unfolding events, in real time. This chronicle captures the experiences of my school community as I recorded them. Hopefully the diary will resonate with school staff and families in every school community across the land. The pandemic was our shared experience: we all faced the same challenges.

I had one basic rule when I wrote the diaries. Parents and staff should not learn about decisions or difficulties from reading the local paper. There should be no shocks, nor confidences breached. It is also not a warts and all diary. I wanted to write an account which would not bring shame or embarrassment to the school. Rather, I wanted to convey the sense of a school community pulling together. Hopefully that is what I have done. So many people have done remarkable things over the past year. Many have simply been remarkable. I think this diary captures that spirit.

Apart from being the very proud Headteacher of this School for the past 20 years, I am also the Secretary of the Essex Branch of the National Association of Headteachers, (NAHT). In this role I attended, along with other Union officials, regular Microsoft Teams meetings with a range of Local Authority Officers, including Clare Kershaw, the Director of Education. In Lockdown 1 the meetings were thrice weekly in Term time and twice weekly in holidays; by Lockdown 3 they were twice weekly in Term times and once-a-week in the holidays. These meetings did give me an insight into, and occasionally influence, how the Local Authority, (LA), was leading Essex schools though the pandemic. Emails I received from a number of the 600+ members of the NAHT gave me an understanding of what issues were keeping fellow headteachers awake at night.

We were having to make it up as we were going along - just like the Government, just like the LA.

Alan Garnett, Headteacher

About North Primary School and Nursery

North Primary School has places for 420 children, with two classes per year group. The Nursery offers 15 hours or 30 hour places for up to 52 three and four-year-olds. The School employs 70 staff.

The local community is wonderfully diverse. We celebrate difference and aim to meet the needs and nurture the interests and talents of all our pupils.

Thanks to our own charity, Free For All, we do not charge for school day trips, swimming lessons and music lessons.

Free For All generates income and creates opportunity by building an enterprise culture within the school and forging strong links locally, nationally and internationally.

More information about the School's present can be found at:
http://northschool.org.uk/

More information about the School's past can be found at:
https://www.northschoolcxxv.com/

FREE FOR ALL

This logo was designed by Connor Crawford, a former pupil and now a highly successful Design Director..

Daily Gazette #ThereWithYou

School life as we had never seen it before

SUNDAY March 22: Parents who qualified as "key workers" or had children in other categories specified by the Government advised in a ParentMail message at 11am of arrangements for the following day.

Uniform to be worn. Registration in the playground. School meals provided. Mixed age classes.

"Staff will plan to make the school day educational but it will be different from usual. Routines will be dependent on the number of staff available."

The weekend heralded the arrival of spring. Mothering Sunday was a sad affair. Elderly mothers were told not to see their children and grandchildren but the glorious sunshine saw large numbers ignore the Government's advice.

Health Secretary Matt Hancock, interviewed on the TV, said that even key workers should now think about whether they had to

● Headteacher Alan Garnett's diary tells how the school moved into unknown territory as it closed to all but the children of key workers and others in need

send their children to school.

Monday March 23: My first email at 8am reinforced the Health Secretary's message. Because we were entering the unknown, all staff were instructed to report for work.

I had shared a draft staffing

> Schools were to continue to remain open to some families but only as a last resort

structure with colleagues over the weekend which I discussed with senior leaders this morning.

Registration in the playground showed that parents had looked again at their childcare needs as only 27 children arrived in school. Up to 70 had been expected.

Once it was confirmed that the staffing was adequate for the day, I briefed remaining staff, gave them a form to complete which would indicate their availability for working during the Easter Holiday and then sent them home. I spent the morning devising a staff rota for the rest of the week.

At 3.30pm I joined a

Daily Gazette, Tuesday 31 March 2020

Introduction

The first three instalments of the diary appeared in the Gazette on March 27th, 30th and 31st 2020. They were ghost-written by Sir Bob Russell.

From Monday March 23rd I started to write the diary myself. Each week's diary was published in the Colchester Daily Gazette the following week.

First article published 27th March

While Coronavirus has seemingly only been a major issue for British people since the beginning of March, for North Primary School it started in January because what has become a crisis in the UK was taking hold in Italy.

For several years North Primary School has been involved in educational projects with other schools across Continental Europe, although the UK has now left the European Union the schools are keen to see the three-year Erasmus project continue.

January - booking the Erasmus visit to Heraklion for March 29th. Italian Erasmus Project Co-ordinators in lockdown ... eventual postponement at the start of March.

February - will the VEX Nationals (robot competition finals in Shropshire) go ahead on February 29th? Yes, but I told the parents up in Telford we would not be going to the USA even if we won - and we did win several awards and would have been eligible to compete in the World Finals in Kentucky in April, again, as in 2019.

Too much uncertainty, other countries on lockdown, the UK were sure to follow. USA was not taking it seriously but would have to soon and a xenophobic President would be making all sorts of decisions. What if we got stuck there? What if one of our group got it out there - their health system is very expensive. Parents and children were very disappointed.

VEX Winners!

VEX winners, Colchester Town Hall balcony

Wednesday 11th March
Reception at Town Hall where Mayor Nick Cope congratulated both the North School boys' and girls' teams for their successes at the robot finals. Afterwards found it had been announced that international school trips from UK cancelled.

On the 12th, VEX cancelled World Finals.

Schools closed across the World but not in UK.

Thursday 12th March
First ParentMail electronic message to parents and carers about Coronavirus, the first of more than 20 in the next seven days!

Friday 13th March
Daily briefings for teachers started following Gov.UK guidance that individuals should commence seven-day self-isolation if they had three symptoms.

Second article published Monday 30th March

Monday 16th March
Daily briefing to teachers at 3.45pm raised the prospect that schools may be asked to remain open during the Easter break to enable health professionals and other important workers to continue to do their jobs. This stunned the teachers but they are an amazing bunch and responded positively to the idea. The PM's briefing at 5pm changed things drastically. Instead of self-isolation for seven days if you had three symptoms, it became 14 days family isolation if you had one of two symptoms. This was a game changer. There were two ParentMail messages sent to parents in reaction to this announcement. This would not only impact on schoolchildren and their families but also staff.

Tuesday 17th March
Four messages with one at 8.07am (before School started) and then three in quick succession at lunchtime. The first of these said that 90 children were absent.

The second was headed Home Learning - with this message:
Teachers have been preparing for the time when schools close. They are thinking of ways to set and share tasks.

The directive for families to self-isolate has caught us out and families who are self-isolating for 14 days are keen for us to send work home electronically.
Teachers will treat this challenge as a priority. Watch this space.

The next message on Tuesday 17th was headed Protecting Staff, and thanked parents for their messages of support. Meetings with parents were cancelled and volunteers stood down; with phone calls between parents and staff rather than face-to-face meetings. Parents requested to *'spread themselves out'* at pick-up time in the playground and all-weather sports area.

Wednesday 18th March
Seven ParentMail messages sent out during the day, the first at 8.05am and the last at 7.29pm. The first, headed Home Learning, said:
Our best wishes to those families in self-isolation. Teachers will start sending work by ParentMail (Years 1-6) or Tapestry either today or Thursday.

The third of the morning said that the School had Foodbank vouchers for families in need.

The Government still wanted schools to remain open but the 14-day family isolation immediately led to schools losing not just pupils but staff too... which of course led to the announcement on Wednesday 18th (at 5pm) that UK schools would close two days later, with Friday 20th the last day. The final message of the day, in the evening, confirmed that the School would close after Friday for most pupils with some exceptions for the children of 'key workers' and other specified categories. All of the above measures were announced by the Secretary of State for Education Gavin Williamson in the House of Commons. He said that the categories of key worker would be announced by the Cabinet Office in the morning of the 19th.

Thursday 19th March

Teachers started to email home learning information via ParentMail messages, the first at 7.41am, specifically for Year 6 with a 'Home Learning Daily Task'. The staff had also created 'home learning packs' comprising an exercise book, plain paper, a pencil, rubber and spelling lists for every child. This was a fantastic effort from all the staff to get this organised so quickly. It was greatly appreciated by parents.

But families and schools were most keen to find out who the key workers would be and how many children we would have to plan for from Monday 23rd. We waited and waited. School phones around the country were ringing constantly as anxious parents needed to know if they would be able to send their children to School or have to make alternative childcare arrangements. Headteachers were geared up to turn this information around quickly. It was a huge frustration to get to the end of the day and still not be told. A whole day of contingency planning was wasted. The key worker document was published by Gov.UK after midnight. It also confirmed that children eligible for Free School Meals should still have a lunch provided even if they were not in School. My working day began at 2.30am to prepare to implement these changes.

Friday 20th March

Six ParentMail messages, the first at 7.31am and the sixth at 5.09pm. Parents advised about how they could keep in touch whilst the School was 'closed'. Another message said that all Before and After School Clubs 'will stop indefinitely after today' including Breakfast, Sunrise and Sunset Clubs. And another advised parents that the 'key worker school place request form' had to be submitted no later than 5pm. Tables were put in the playground for parents to fill the forms in on arrival at School to speed up the process. These plus emailed forms received during the day amounted to approximately 70 pupils. Parents returned their Free School Meal request forms. They had to indicate whether they could collect, if they would be sending somebody else as the family were isolating or if there was simply no way they could collect, volunteers would deliver. All staff were briefed at 3.45pm about how School would open on the 23rd. Staff were advised to keep checking their emails over the weekend.

The PM announced at 5.00pm that this would be the last night that pubs and restaurants would be open. He urged people to adhere to social distancing rules.

Third article published March 31st
Sunday 22nd March

Parents who qualified as '*key workers*' or had children in other categories specified by the Government advised in a ParentMail message at 11am of arrangements for the following day. Uniform to be worn. Registration in the playground. School meals provided. Mixed age classes. '*Staff will plan to make the school day educational but it will be different from usual. Routines will be dependent on the number of staff available.*'

The weekend heralded the arrival of Spring. Mothering Sunday was a sad affair. Elderly mothers were told not to see their children and grandchildren but the glorious sunshine saw large numbers ignore the Government's advice. Deaths in Italy and Spain spiked and the number of deaths in the UK increased too.

Matt Hancock, Health Minister, interviewed on the TV said that even key workers should now think about whether they had to send their children to school.

Articles by Alan Garnett
Monday 23rd March

My first email at 8.00am reinforced the Minister's message that only as a last resort should children be sent to School. However because we were entering the unknown all staff were instructed to report for work. I had shared a draft staffing structure with colleagues over the weekend which I discussed with Senior Leaders at 8.00am.

Registration in the playground showed that parents had looked again at their childcare needs as only 27 children arrived in School. Once it was confirmed that the staffing was adequate for the day I briefed remaining staff, gave them a form to complete which would indicate their availability for working during the Easter Holiday and then sent them home. I spent the morning devising a staff rota for the rest of the week.

At 3.30pm I joined a conference call, in my role as Secretary of Essex National Association of Headteachers (NAHT), with other Union officials and Local Authority representatives. This was very constructive. I bashed out the notes to circulate to NAHT members, in the knowledge that the PM's 5.00pm briefing may make those notes irrelevant.

Which it did, largely, but we had to wait until 8.30pm when the PM made an Address to the Nation informing us that we were on lockdown for three weeks and the Police would arrest anybody breaking the rules of social distancing. Schools were to continue to remain open to some families but only as a last resort.

Tuesday 24th March
The country is now on Lockdown.
14 pupils today.

The LA still has overall responsibility for what happens in our schools but has had its ability to do this severely restricted over the last ten years. And whilst I believe strongly that schools need a LA to co-ordinate provision etc, I have not always been in agreement with how it does this. However Director of Education, Clare Kershaw, and her team have worked tirelessly to keep schools informed and supported literally 24/7. The LA has been responsive to our concerns and given good advice in interpreting Government directives which have been released often in a less than timely fashion and without the absolute clarity required.

This morning's email from Clare Kershaw included the news that she would be exploring the idea of 'clustering schools', merging available staff into one school to teach pupils still allowed to attend. This is not popular with heads and teachers. It would increase the amount of movement and contact across communities which seems contrary to the aim of lockdown, to eliminate contact and disease-spread. Staff are happy to work in their own schools, less keen to work in others and the pupils themselves, many of whom are vulnerable, would struggle in a different setting. But Clare's final email of the day announced that she would not impose one model on schools and leave us to sort out our own solutions if we are happy and had the staff capacity. We are happy.

I put out a Newsline today, the seventh edition this month, and it was full of love - emails and photos from parents and staff, describing what they are doing and how they are feeling about this 'new normal'. Let's hope we can maintain this positivity.

Wednesday 25th March
Only eight pupils today.

We continue to provide 'grab and go' packed lunches for children not in School but eligible for Free School Meals. We will continue to do this until the Government launches its e-voucher system. A few inquiries with the LA and NAHT uncover that the scheme will be rolled out on Monday 30th. Details will follow apparently.

We often curse social media for many of its negative influences but it is proving a force for good so far as are all the forms of electronic communication. Parents and staff are actually reading what I send out! We have received some lovely emails from parents which we are sharing through our newsletters. And links to Facebook pages and websites are giving people lots of ideas and support.

Thursday 26th March
12 pupils today.

We are scaling back the number of staff we have working with the children but we still need other non-teaching roles to continue. It is the busiest time of the year for the office. They have to sort out financial year-end, tie-up new contracts and put the new budget on the system. On top of this they have had to introduce new Covid-19 related attendance record systems for Essex County Council and the Government. For reasons of self-isolation, we are down to only one member of the kitchen team able to work. Fingers crossed she and her family remain healthy until her colleagues can return. Many schools are struggling with their cleaning contractors for a variety of Covid-19 reasons - from staff shortage to shortage of supplies. We are very lucky. We have The Hughes Corporation. Pete and Mary Hughes are husband and wife so can work without worrying about the two metre rule. They are making sure the School is sparkle-clean. Go Team North!

More good news to cheer up everybody, thanks to Firstsite art gallery. Cliqq, a local media company, has made a film of a day in the life of our Reception classes which we planned to show to our September 2020 starters in May. That is looking unlikely. So, we will be holding the Film's Premiere in September for the 60 little stars of the film, and families too of course, in the Firstsite cinema. We will all dress to impress, there will be paparazzi and an after-party. Something special to look forward to.

Friday 27th March
11 pupils today.

I received an email last night. Here is a bit of it -

As we are drawing near to the first week of closure (non closure) I just wanted to say a big thank you. It just helped me so much knowing that you were all looking after [my daughter] and happy to do so I could then do my job as a nurse and help the system without worrying about her. A big thank you to all the staff that have been in this week too with their creative teaching, play and food. North is so community orientated and all of us that have children there are very lucky.

I shared this message with staff who then went out into their streets at 8.00pm to clap and cheer for the NHS with even more passion. Emails like that are a clear reminder of how vital the NHS is at the present time.

A delivery arrived today from Carli Norris, parent, actor and entrepreneur. She has made face masks for staff. What a lovely gesture. Greatly appreciated.

Applause for teachers is deserved

MONDAY April 6

Officially the first day of the school Easter holidays. I have blocked out a four week period – which started last week - making sure all staff have their contractual two weeks annual leave but it is very difficult for them to switch off knowing the school is open. Teachers have eased up on the home learning. Parents have been provided with ideas and links which they can use if they want.

11 pupils today. Boris Johnson was admitted to hospital last night. Over the weekend Government ministers threatened the lockdown may have to go further if small but significant numbers of people continued to flout the new laws. Michael Gove surprised everybody when he announced the free school

■ Applause - Prime Minister Boris Johnson claps

 In his latest diary instalment, Alan Garnett, head teacher of North Primary School in Colchester, tells of uncertainty for schools during the coronavirus lockdown

' It is anticipated the longer lockdown and school closure continue, the greater strain on family life

Monday 30th March

British Summer Time is here. Its arrival was heralded with hail and sleet yesterday. Ice on the windscreen.

10 pupils today. The children gave TV's keep fit Joe Wicks a day off and began the morning with a workout to Cosmic Yoga. She has daily themes and today was FROZEN, which went down very well with the younger girls.

On arrival in School, it was good to open emails sent in over the weekend. Lots of busy families. Another email was received from Susan Sydenham from Eld Lane Baptist Church. Year 6s would have been visiting there this week for their Easter Cracked event. The Church also very generously give every Year 6 pupil in their final Term a book called, *It's Your Move.* She said she will make sure they still receive a copy although it is increasingly unlikely that she will be able to give it to them in person in School. Just one other element of their rite of passage to secondary school they will miss.

Today was the day the Government had promised to announce their e-voucher scheme for all children eligible for Free School Meals, (FSM). Frustratingly schools have been waiting all day for the news. In this evening's daily email to Essex schools, Clare Kershaw, Director of Education, wrote to inform schools that no information had been received.

Tuesday 31st March

Overnight the DfE announced its FSM e-voucher scheme. It was worth the wait. It appears to be a very impressive and generous scheme. The scheme will make available to the adult with caring responsibility for that child a weekly e-voucher to the value of £15 per child redeemable in most supermarkets. Any family without email will be posted an e-Gift card. Administering this scheme will create a lot of work for school office staff but it will be worth it. We need to wait for the software company who will co-ordinate the system to get in touch, we need to check our FSM records, make contact with all families directly who do not have access to the internet. Then we can set it up ready for the start of the Summer Term when it goes live. (The scheme does not cover school holidays). This will also give families more time to register for FSM. Sadly, many more families are now being sucked into the Benefit system and this scheme will be extremely helpful whilst lockdown continues.

I do have one concern. We currently have universal Free School Meals for all children up to the age of seven. This scheme does not include this. There was talk at the time of the Budget last month that the Government wanted to end universal Free School Meals. That did not happen but let us hope this is not a sneaky way of achieving that aim.

More sad news. Two members of staff have family members (not in their households though) who have tested positive for Covid-19. The good news is they are not very ill but it is a sign of things to come - not many families are going to escape this pandemic without having someone close to them contract this disease.

Wednesday 1st April

Email with instructions for the Free School Meal scheme arrived at lunchtime. Office staff can now get on with setting the system up ready for its introduction on April 20th. Phone calls start to be made to make sure all the eligible families are on board. Still waiting to find out if schools will remain open on Good Friday and Easter Monday. Staff are prepared; they and the parents just need to be told.

Thursday 2nd April

The day started well. We received an email from a parent. Her children left the school about six years ago. They now live in Canada:

I hope you remember us as you all have always been in our thoughts throughout the years. We wanted to send out an email and wish you all well and are keeping safe during these difficult times. Our time at North was filled with many fond times and memories made by your amazing staff. Please keep safe and know we're thinking of you all at North.

Proof that you never forget a teacher.

The day ended well. This afternoon I sent a letter and slide show to all the children (via their parents) and messages are coming back already. In the first, the mum wrote of how the art work her daughters had done has brightened up their home and that the girls had made a cake for their poorly brother to cheer him up. She finished by writing:

Sending lots of love to everyone at North, you are all doing an amazing job and quite frankly I'm not sure we would be getting through this as easily if it wasn't for the wonderful staff sending daily Tapestry (an interactive App.) and emails so thank you.

I taught her husband in the late 90s. He has never forgiven me for making him play centre-half in the school team. He fancied himself as a centre forward. As I say, you never forget a teacher.

Friday 3rd April

Today would normally be the last day of Term. It always begins with a special Easter Parade assembly. The children come to school in their home-made Easter bonnets, caps, hats, fascinators, whatever. It is amazing. They all parade in the hall. It is quite a spectacle. The North School Association (NSA - our parent teacher association) gives every child a little egg and a special guest has the impossible job of choosing winners for every age group. Also, in the assembly Governors present awards to children who have been commended for their outstanding achievement through the term. And we stand and applaud our Colchester Half Marathon Team who proudly show off their medals. Not this year, of course. North is a community school and assemblies like these make that community spirit visible and real for the children. The children are still making their bonnets and sending in photos which I will share via the newsletter. But it won't be the same.

Easter Parade, 2019

Lockdown Easter Parade, 2020

Monday 6th April

Officially the first day of the School Easter Holidays. I have blocked out a four-week period - which started last week - making sure all staff have their contractual two weeks annual leave but it is very difficult for them to switch off knowing the School is open. Teachers have eased up on the home learning. Parents have been provided with ideas and links which they can use if they want.

11 pupils today.

The Prime Minister Boris Johnson was admitted to hospital last night. Over the weekend Government Ministers threatened that the lockdown may have to go further if small but significant numbers of people continued to flout the new laws. Michael Gove surprised everybody when he announced the Free School Meals (FSM) voucher scheme would now be available to families during the holiday. Nothing official came in overnight to confirm this. If it is true then this will catch a lot of schools out and probably Edenred, the company managing the scheme, too. They are already struggling to process all the applications.

Tuesday 7th April

10 pupils today. Big news overnight. Firstly, Boris Johnson's health worsened and he was moved to Intensive Care. The Department for Education (DfE) announce the voucher scheme will apply from yesterday! Good news for families. What schools have still not been told is whether they have to open on the Bank Holidays, now only three days away. Plenty of staff have volunteered. We are planning to be open if parents need us but, so far, all those families still sending their children to School have informed us that they won't need to on those two days.

Ray Gooding, Essex County Council Cabinet Member for Education and Skills, has written a letter to all Essex schools' staff which I passed on to our team. It was a lovely letter and he was keen to point out that school staff are key workers and at 8.00pm on Thursdays the nation are applauding our efforts too in providing a valuable service to our country's most valuable key workers - hospital staff.

The difficulty that this Covid-19 crisis has shown is that despite the adversity, the lack of guidance and information, the manner and speed with which schools and the teaching profession have responded is exemplary. Schools have never been closed in this manner and the teaching profession have never needed to react to such a constantly changing situation. I salute you all for the way you have reacted. ... So, most of all I want to say a big 'THANK YOU' for everything you are doing and next week for the Thursday Clap I will be bequeathing three of every four claps for schools and teachers!

Wednesday 8th April

Five pupils today. This morning the Government finally made its decision on whether schools should be open on the Bank Holidays. The answer is *yes please*, if key workers need it. All the prevarication has meant parents have got it covered.

The message of the day from the LA is what schools need to put in place for the Summer Term to keep in touch with all families. It is anticipated that the longer lockdown and school closure continue, the greater strain on family life. Tragically this will include coping with bereavement for many. How can schools support all our families remotely? That is the challenge we face. Other agencies - such as Social Care, the Emotional Wellbeing and Mental Health Service, school nurses and health visitors - all will be expected to work with schools and families.

These services have reduced their reach over the past years because their capacity has been reduced. All professionals feel frustration at this. How will they cope over the next few months with this additional expectation in supporting more families through this crisis?

Thursday 9th April

I woke up this morning to see that the print and TV media are running four main stories which are creating a feeling of confusion. Boris Johnson remains in intensive care and there is a concern that big decisions will not be made until he has recovered which could take weeks; yesterday the highest number of deaths in the UK were recorded - 938; as the Bank Holiday weekend approaches there is a fear of social distancing being breached on a large scale so there could be an increase of lockdown restrictions, and finally there is talk of schools re-opening. How are schools and families to make sense of all that? Where is the logic in opening schools during a lockdown? I am all for getting back to normal but not before the risk has been managed successfully.

The FSM voucher scheme has hit the national headlines today for all the wrong reasons, prompting Clare Kershaw, Director for Education, to write a letter to all Essex families explaining that Edenred, the company managing the scheme are really struggling and it is not the school's fault if families have not received their e-voucher codes yet. They are not coping.

Friday 10th April

Good Friday. The School does not need to open today. A long weekend of sunshine to look forward to. Will enough people show self-discipline and not make matters worse? France banned outdoor exercise earlier in the week. Let us hope it does not need to come to that here.

Tuesday 14th April
Bank Holiday over. Typical. Apart from it being cold yesterday, the weather has been amazing. It usually rains sideways over the Easter weekend.

Our parents who are key workers cover the spectrum of essential activities - supermarkets, hospitals and care workers. We have a large number of parents who are care workers. This sector hit the news over the long weekend as the sheer number of deaths of elderly people in these homes came to light. Apparently, the care workers are having even more difficulty than hospital workers in getting personal protective equipment (PPE). If hospitals and care homes are not getting the PPE, there seems to be little hope of special schools getting what they need, less chance still for mainstream schools, many of whom have pupils with complex needs.

Five pupils today. The issue of Free School Meal vouchers has not gone away. Office staff are fielding phone calls from frustrated parents who are either still waiting for their vouchers, or, when they have them discover that supermarkets don't recognise their e-voucher codes.

We are told by the Government that numbers of infected people are plateauing, although deaths are rising. The nation is being applauded for abiding by the lockdown measures - instrumental in the fall in new cases, they say. But there are more voices suggesting schools should re-open soon, or if not soon, then open in August.

Wednesday 15th April
Six pupils today. Denmark announce that primary schools are re-opening for some pupils but social distancing rules will still apply. Will this add to the clamour to re-open in this country? It is being characterised as the lives vs. livelihood debate. A crude distinction but it makes the point. We had the chance to learn from other countries who were affected by Covid-19 before us and it looks like we reacted too late. We have the chance to learn from these countries. Let's make better use of this opportunity this time. Denmark is making the slow return to normality having locked down earlier and having had a much lower infection rate and death count. Scientists have always warned against the second wave of infections. Please let us not rush these decisions.

Thursday 16th April
Six pupils today. And today is the day that parents of three and four-year-olds have been waiting for since January. Has their child got a place at the first place preference school in September? We have 60 places. Fifty-three places have been offered to first preferences, seven to second preferences. Let's hope that those seven come to realise that we aren't really second best. We would normally be inviting all these parents to a meeting in May where we tell the new families

what the induction programme is and our Nursery families what the transition arrangements are. There will have to be a re-think this year.

Safeguarding - at its most critical it means child protection but it is an umbrella term covering all aspects of pastoral care. Increasingly, we talk about mental health too. The Government is rightly concerned about the welfare of children and their families at this time. Sent down the command chain are '*guidelines*' on keeping in touch with our children and families. An excellent ambition but full of complex challenges. Schools have already developed good communication systems and have set up interactive learning platforms but will be expected to keep logs of all contact on a weekly basis. That is a lot of phone calls and a lot of emails. On the plus side the teachers are looking forward to talking to the children in their classes.

Friday 17th April
Nine pupils today. It was announced last night that the lockdown will continue for a further three weeks at least. But the re-opening of schools remains a subject of interest to the media. BBC Essex Radio want to cover it in their Monday Breakfast Show.

Wrote to all the parents today to inform them that teachers will be calling them next week. In theory it is the start of the Summer Term. A busy time of sponsored runs, trips, tests, fêtes concerts, swimming lessons, sports days and much more. The only event not at risk is the writing of the children's annual report although it could be based on only half-a-year of schooling.

Monday 20th April 2020

Over the weekend, Izy, a pupil in Year 5 cheered everybody up. She has launched an appeal to raise money for the local hospital trust. She will draw bespoke flowers in exchange for a donation. But, she has said that if people are struggling and can't donate, she is happy to draw them a flower to help cheer them up. How wonderful is that.

Izy Werenowska

Monday has been a very eventful day. It should have been the first day of the Summer Term which it was for 14 pupils. It started with a radio interview on BBC Essex and finished with a television appearance on BBC Look East on the subject of the re-opening of schools. Over the weekend journalists were allegedly briefed '*off the record*' by some Ministers about the possibility of schools reopening on May 11th.

Gavin Williamson, Secretary of State for Education, led Sunday's Government Press Conference in order to rule that out. He went further, announcing that disadvantaged Year 10s would get laptops and connectivity. That is not a short -term measure. It would suggest schools will be closed for a while. If the experience of the confusion and delay with the school meal voucher scheme is anything to go by, these Year 10s may be getting laptops in their Christmas stockings.

My radio interview lasted about two minutes - by Sonia Watson, a former North pupil, and I did about three minutes worth of recording for the TV, which I was told would be edited down to about 15 seconds! I was worried that my message would not be represented clearly so I sent an email to parents:

When Will Schools Re-open for Everybody?

This continual speculation is not helpful. All we do know is that the country is in lockdown for three more weeks and the situation will be reviewed at the end of that period. My position can be summarised as follows:

I believe that schools should re-open only when the Government's Five Tests have been met. We should wait to learn from other countries ahead of us on their road to recovery.

The real hardships and difficulties many families are experiencing should not be for nothing. If we rush to re-open schools, we risk a second wave Covid crisis. This must be avoided.

The country is a long way off meeting those five tests. In the meantime, all the staff at North will continue to do everything we can to:

1. Provide a clean, safe environment for our key workers' children.
2. Provide remote interactive study programmes.
3. Support children's emotional health through a remote pastoral care network.

As it happened the most remarked upon aspect of my 15 seconds of fame was my hair! And I was in much need of a haircut on March 23rd.

The rest of the day was spent in phone conversation with every teacher – 26 in total. This week they will be ringing every parent to Keep in Touch and check all is well with the home learning. All children have access rights to interactive learning platforms now and it is important that parents are confident with them. The teachers will speak to every child too, hopefully. It is a major logistical operation. Teachers will be making these calls from home, and will obviously withhold their own number. So they will email parents on the day that they will call so that the parents know to expect a call from a private number.

Tuesday 21st April
15 pupils today.

Some of the teachers have started calling parents. This is a typical email that was sent in advance.

Mr Garnett sent an email last week explaining that teachers will be phoning parents this week to touch base. I am really looking forward to contacting you. I will be phoning from 9.30am today and it will take approximately 3 and a half hours to contact you all. I will work alphabetically using the first names that the children use in class. I am using my mobile and it will show up on your phone as a PRIVATE number. It will be lovely to be able to say hello to the children and yourselves. Take care and I look forward to getting in touch today.

Team work at North has always been a strength and colleagues are working hard to maintain that spirit through group communication. A good example of this came through at the end of the day. Teachers who had made their calls shared their experiences with others by email. Here is an example.

Just to let you all know that I contacted all my class today by phone and it was lovely!! The children all responded brilliantly and it really felt as if they had been waiting for my call since I emailed this morning. There was also a real sense of gratitude from the parents - they all wanted to chat and check that all of us are OK. They really appreciate all that we are doing for their children but at the same time want us to be safe and well and wanted this message shared with all teachers.

This was really worthwhile doing and an added bonus - there was a lot of activity on SeeSaw (the online learning platform) for the rest of the day!

What teachers are finding is that although families are finding lockdown hard, they support it and are appreciative of everything the teachers are doing. Our parent body have the greatest respect for the teachers, rightly so. Some parents, apparently, were even suggesting that teachers deserve a pay rise. I am sure the teachers would not have made that up!

Wednesday 22nd April
These phone calls are bound to throw up some problems. 450 children. Over 250 families. What do we do if a teacher cannot make contact with a parent and they

do not respond to emails either? Teachers are teachers, what if struggling? Are they qualified to advise or even able to help? Pa issued with a range of contact details - Foodbank, housing, Free S vouchers. Teachers can signpost parents where necessary. Beyond that co will be referred to me.

St. George's Day tomorrow. I think a dragon may make an appearance in School today. Let's hope there is a brave knight at hand to slay the creature and keep the children and staff safe.

Thursday 23rd April
A day spent in communication with teachers giving me feedback on their phone calls to families. The vast majority of parents and children seem to be coping and getting to grips with home learning. Inevitably there have been some tough conversations, particularly with families struggling to cope with bereavement or very ill relatives. Some parents have been hard to reach. Others are encountering problems. This has led to a range of actions: further conversations with some parents and also home visits – social distancing observed of course; emails to family support workers; conversations with the school nurse; the school special needs co-ordinator and social and emotional health co-ordinators; the Head of Child First (the school is a member of this charitable trust which provides a range of services for families and young people) to discuss remote counselling support, and conversations with social care.

Friday 24th April
10 pupils today.

Testing key workers for Covid-19 has been a massive issue. It was announced yesterday that all key workers can apply to be tested at local test centres. Our nearest is at the Ipswich Park and Ride. This will be helpful to so many school staff across the country who are isolating because they or their household members are *symptomatic*.

, sent me their Year group weekly newsletters.
ensive record of the School's first week of fully
eek where teachers made direct contact by phone
child. A new milestone in the School's 125 years
WWII the School remained open for all its pupils.
ded to the School's rich archive.
on returned to work today.

unique. But all parents have to respond to similar demands.
Feeu   in the house, maintain routine, keep them occupied and help
them make   of a scary situation which has no clear and obvious end. Nobody
in School underestimates that challenge. School staff face those same pressures in
their own homes too. They face the same pressures of parents working from home
juggling work and family life.

In contacting families, in setting home learning, in their communications with
children and parents staff are trying to educate, nurture and support. That is a
massive task, one that we will never be able to say we have got right for all families
all the time but the teachers are doing a pretty amazing job of it so far. Judging by
their comments, our families recognise this achievement too. And not just parents.
Cassie, who is 10, wrote this letter to all the staff.

*Thank you for keeping work going and supporting the children and thank you for keeping
the children educated. In this time we need you more than ever because you are making
sure the children carry on even though we are not at School. Thank you for calling us to
make sure we are OK and for making sure everything is fine at home and not only are we
doing well but our family is too. I really appreciate you are here for us when we need you
the most.*

Thank you, Cassie.

I had a tricky decision to make today. The Royal College of Nursing has asked the
nation to pause for a minute's silence at 11.00am in recognition of the hospital and
care workers who have died from Covid-19. A number in the region of 100. That is
100 too many and a minute's silence is the least the nation can do. However, nearly
all the children attending School have parents who work in hospitals or care homes.
Some of these children are as young as five. We know that the children are worried
about their parents going to work every day. It did not seem right to bring this
real danger to the forefront of their minds. Kitchen and office staff respected the
minute's silence. I thought it better that these children did not, better instead for
the children to celebrate their parent's bravery at 8.00pm every Thursday evening.

Wednesday 29th April

It is not only the lessons and playtimes that the children are missing. Schools provide a whole range of before school, lunchtime and after-school clubs. These clubs give the children so many other opportunities to develop their interests and talents. So, one of our Learning Support Assistants is launching NORVAC - The North Virtual Astronomy Club. Another first for the School.

Gavin Williamson, Secretary of State for Education, questioned by the House of Commons Education Select Committee, said that he was looking into plans to partially re-open schools whilst social distancing rules remain in place. But that may only apply to England. Scotland and Wales may make their own decision. Ministers in Northern Ireland are suggesting that schools will not re-open there until September because they think parents won't send their children to school yet.

Thursday 30th April

I have had some conversations with families whose children could come to School. They are reluctant to send them because they worry that their children might catch Covid-19. Some of these families are struggling with their children at home but I perfectly understand their anxiety. I cannot in all conscience offer the assurance that if they send their children to School, they will not catch this disease, despite everything we are doing. The School is sparkle clean. The children are spread out. Now we have 15 in School every day we are holding indoor PE (physical education) sessions for half at a time - in a big hall - so that they can keep their two metre distancing. That is a good example of the challenge we face when re-opening.

Boris Johnson led the daily Press Conference for the first time since his illness. He announced that detailed plans would be published next week for the phased re-opening of schools.

This evening the Governors met, remotely, for the first time ever. We not only discussed what partial re-opening could look like but also what School will look like in September. There is so much focus on June, little thought seems to have gone into what schools will look like in September.

Friday 1st May

I placed an order today with the Local Authority for all children with a social worker to receive a laptop to help with their home learning. They are expected to arrive in June.

Sums do not add up on social distancing

● **North Primary School head teacher Alan Garnett** shares part of his latest diary instalment on life on the chalk face during the coronavirus pandemic including instructions from Government for some pupils to return

MONDAY May 11
Last night the nation sat down at 7pm to wait for the PM's address on how we would be led out of lockdown. Schools would be told to allow more pupils back from June 1. It was time for the detail. The previous Sunday the PM had announced Year 6 would be a priority. Check. Then he said reception and Year1 pupils should come back too. Where did that come from? And the details? To follow in the week. Frustrating.

This morning a Government document revealed there was another priority group – pre-schoolers. We have 50 Nursery children, 60 Reception (five-year-olds), 60 Year 1s and 60 Year 6s. Social distancing will remain the rule for interaction. Still no details. However, I am allowing no more than ten children in a classroom to try to adhere to the 2m rule. I will need 23 classrooms for these children. I have 14.

The school newsletter was sent home this morning. It included the names of our first Home Learners of the Week. In the absence of assemblies where Good Work and Good Citizen awards are presented, teachers will nominate their home learner of the week.

At 4pm a Government document is finally released, laying out the expectations and guidance. It acknowledges young children cannot social distance but if the Government's five tests have been met they should come back to school on June 1. The main recommendation is 15 children maximum in a class. Not in our classrooms.

I will plan for ten. The children must remain in their groups with the same teacher and they must be kept apart from other groups throughout the school day to limit the risk of spreading the virus.

Year 6 would have started their SATs today. Some will be relieved, some will be disappointed that they did not get the chance to show how much they have learnt at North.

Tuesday May 12
More information and advice from the Government. Apparently they are still being guided by the science but now it is down to our common sense to get to Phase 2. I was never very good at science at school; in fact after some disastrous mocks I acquired the nickname Albert in honour of Albert Einstein. I have a vague memory of being taught Newton's Laws of Motion and particle theory. I don't remember studying a science module called Common Sense. Keyboard warriors are saying it is time for teachers to stand up and be counted. They are already being counted -23 teachers have died from Covid-19 already across the country. The risk to the safety of children and staff has to be assessed properly.

Wednesday May 13
Have drafted plan to accommodate all the children in government priority order whilst continuing to have places for key worker children and vulnerable children.

The plan is published. Parents of our youngest pupils receive an acceptance offer letter which explains what school will look like for their children. They will be able to make a fully informed choice. I do state it is a conditional offer dependent on the Government go ahead and also having the staff I need to implement the plan. Parents have a choice – they will not be fined for not sending their children to school.

Friday May 15
The union leaders' meeting with Chris Whitty, Chief Medical Officer, did not prove to be a defining moment. Doubts remain.Like all schools, we will continue to "do our duty", as we have been since March 23 and watch the national debate.

> The recommendation is 15 children in a class. Not in our classrooms. I will plan for ten

Thursday May 14

Monday 4th May 2020

Over the weekend I was texting a friend who is a Head in one of the Gulf States. They shut schools to every pupil a couple of weeks ahead of the UK. He was saying how parental perceptions are changing. He said that his parents are notoriously hard to please and a lot of his time is taken up addressing their complaints. Since lockdown he said he has received nothing but compliments from parents. He also reported that his teachers are working flat out managing the home learning. He has also just been told that the schools will receive one day inspections on how they are managing remote learning as they will remain closed until September.

The rest of the weekend was taken up digesting the latest speculation from Westminster on the phased opening up of schools to more pupils. We were told the PM will make an announcement on Sunday 10th May.

I sent a survey to Year 6 parents today. This is part of the accompanying letter:

I think it is really important that the Government, the Local Authority and schools find out what parents are thinking at this really difficult time. Speculation about re-opening continues and seems to get louder every weekend. The PM will announce his plans for schools next Sunday. In the meantime, newspapers are being briefed that the PM is keen for Y6 to return on June 1st. I would like you to consider this scenario and complete a survey for the Governors.

The survey asks for the parents' views on their concerns around school closure and when they think the time is right for their children to return to school.

21 children in School today. The most since lockdown. I have offered places to a few families who are suffering bereavements. We have two excellent social and emotional health co-ordinators who will help these children.

Tuesday 5th May

Had a conference call with colleagues in Italy, Greece and Finland. The project, sponsored by the EU Erasmus fund, to devise teaching tools for children with dyslexia has obviously been seriously affected by school closure and travel restrictions. The project will conclude remotely at the end of September. Italian Universities are not allowing travel in or out of the country before Christmas. Speaking to the Italian Directeur, she told me that teachers are working flat out there too. It should come as no surprise really that teacher workload is incredibly high. Teachers are also facing the same pressures as all working families: juggling work and family life and making sure their own children do their home learning.

Wednesday 6th May

The Office Manager, Amanda Sancassani, has not been sleeping well. She has been worrying about the families who should be receiving shopping vouchers and still have not. This is common across the country. She has been on the phone constantly to the scheme administrators and to parents helping them through a hugely frustrating application process. To make sure that these families do not have to wait any longer for the system to work for them she has bought supermarket gift cards. The School will reimburse her and claim the money from the Government in due course.

I have been in continual discussion with Heads around the county on the conditions for opening schools to more pupils. We have so many questions that need answering. Let us hope the Government has carefully considered what is the scientific and medical reasoning underpinning the precise timing of the 'phased re-opening' and that they share this with the country. We also need to know what the Government wants to happen beyond Day 1: we need to see their route map through June, July, August and September so that we can plan effectively and keep our families and pupils fully informed and gain their confidence.

Thursday 7th May

I collated the parent survey results today. They are mixed. It is clear that parents want their children to have the chance to complete their final term in primary but know that even if they do return, it won't be the kind of experience they would have had. Most significantly they are split on when they would want their children to return to School. A third say June, a third July and a third would rather wait until September. The Government has a confidence test to pass here if they want parents to send their children back to school in June.

VE Day tomorrow. Let's enjoy that celebration and then wait for Sunday's announcement.

Monday 11th May

What a weekend! It started with a Bank Holiday, moved to the Friday to tie in with the 75th anniversary of VE Day. This would have been a major event in the School forming one more exciting chapter in the history of the oldest State School in Colchester. This is our 125th anniversary and thanks to the brilliant inspiration and sheer hard work of Project Co-ordinator Laura Davison and Historian Claire Driver, our CXXV project continues to live and breathe. Although we were not able to host veterans last week and hold a street party, Laura and Claire have captured the memories of these former pupils over the course of this year on our special CXXV website (www.northschoolcxxv.com). Their memories of attending North during WWII, experiencing air raids, rationing, VE Day, and, interestingly - home schooling contribute to a superb archive.

VE Day poster by Gaia

Last night the nation sat down at 7.00pm to wait for the PM's address on how we would be led out of Lockdown. The headlines had been heavily leaked. Schools would be told to allow more pupils back from June 1st. It was time for the detail. The previous Sunday the PM had announced that Year 6 would be a priority. Check. Then he said Reception and Year 1 pupils should come back too. Where did that come from? And the details? To follow in the week. Frustrating. In the meantime, we no longer have to Stay Safe in England, we have to Stay Alert. The other Home Nations will continue to Stay Safe.

This morning a Government document revealed that there was another priority group - pre-schoolers. We have 50 Nursery children, 60 Reception (five-year-olds), 60 Year 1's and 60 Year 6's. Social distancing will remain the rule for interaction. Still no details. However, I do have a maths problem. I am allowing no more than 10 children in a classroom to try to adhere to the 2m rule. I will need 23 classrooms for these children. I have 14! Cancelled the Governor meeting scheduled for the evening to discuss the Government proposals. Deferred to Wednesday evening.

The School newsletter was sent home this morning. It included the names of our very first Home Learners of the Week. In the absence of assemblies where Good Work and Good Citizen Awards are presented, and the impossibility of hosting tea parties to celebrate pupil excellence and contribution to the School, teachers will nominate their home learner of the week. Seven teachers each week will do this –one class from each year group. I spent the afternoon speaking to the children and their parents on the phone. One of the nominee's was Aron, whose parents both work at the hospital. They work opposite shifts and have kept their children off school, even though they are obviously key workers, because they decided the safest way to avoid getting the virus and not being able to work was to keep the children at home. Many frontline workers have done the same. Well, Aron was nominated not just because he is doing lots of school work but for being a superstar around the house too, helping out with the chores. It was good to talk to the children and forget about the logistical problems I will have to solve.

At 4.00pm a Government document is finally released, laying out the Government expectations and guidance. It acknowledges that young children cannot social distance but if the Government's five test have been met, they should come back to school on June 1st. The main recommendation is 15 children maximum in a class. Not in our classrooms. I will plan for 10. The children must remain in their groups with the same teacher and they must be kept apart from other groups throughout the school day to limit the risk of spreading the virus. This will mean not every 'bubble' will have a teacher, their learning will be led by assistants and nursery nurses. We have brilliant support staff but that is a big responsibility.

Year 6 would have started their SATs today. Some will be relieved, some will be disappointed that they did not get the chance to show how much they have learnt at North.

Tuesday 12th May

More information and advice from the Government. Apparently, they are still being guided by the science but now it is down to our common sense to get to phase 2. I was never very good at science at school; in fact, after some disastrous GCSE mocks I acquired the nickname Albert in honour of Albert Einstein. I have a vague memory of being taught Newton's Laws of Motion and Particle Theory. I don't remember studying a science module called Common Sense!

Media are all over the proposals. Keyboard warriors are saying it is time for teachers to stand up and be counted. They are already being counted - 23 teachers have died from Covid-19 already across the country. The Unions are not happy. They want to see the real science behind the decision making. I agree. The risk to the safety of children and staff has to be assessed properly.

Wednesday 13th May
Have drafted a plan to accommodate all the children in Government priority order whilst continuing to have places for key worker children and vulnerable children. The plan can accommodate Nursery, Reception, Year 1. There is no room for Year 6s. Two and a quarter hour Zoom Governors' meeting this evening, grilling my plans. The Governors' questions covered all aspects: the safety of children, the safety of staff and the logistics. Parents will be informed in the morning.

Thursday 14th May
Before I publish the plan, I feel it incumbent to break the bad news to Year 6, who were under the impression that they would be invited back first. I am sure that many of them will be shocked, disappointed and possibly even angry about this. Those feelings would be understandable. It is a very sad way for them to end their primary school career. The Government plan says that if a school cannot accommodate all its priority pupils, then it should ask a neighbouring school. I have written to all the secondary schools to see if they will increase their transition offer to these children who will soon be their students.

The plan is published. Parents of our youngest pupils receive an acceptance offer letter which explains what School will look like for their children. They will be able to make a fully informed choice. I do state that it is a conditional offer - dependent on the Government go ahead and also having the staff I need to implement the plan. Parents have a choice - they will not be fined for not sending their children to School. Some staff have no choice - they are unable to return to work. The others will have a choice. All employees across the land are being told that if their place of work is not safe, they do not have to cross that threshold. The Unions have an audience with the Government's scientific advisors tomorrow. Will they be reassured. Local Authorities are getting involved. They want to know whether they have the power to tell schools not to open based on regional differences in the R (reproduction) number and infection and death rates.

Friday 15th May
We usually celebrate the end of SATs Week with North's Got Talent, (NGT). The Year 6 School Councillors organise and lead the whole thing. Not this year. But the teachers have kept the spirit of NGT alive with a video show. Each class will have a winner and their videos will be put on the School website. Mary, one of our cleaners, an artist in her spare time, will be the judge.

The Union leaders' meeting with Professor Chris Whitty, Chief Medical Officer, did not prove to be a defining moment. Doubts remain apparently. Unexpectedly, the British Medical Association has gone on record as saying June 1st is too soon. Wait until June 15th is their advice. Liverpool's Local Authority has declared their schools will not re-open on June 1st.

School Offer forms are trickling in. No wonder. Are parents hesitant to reply? Are they waiting to learn more? If the biggest brains in the country cannot reach agreement, how do we know what is the right thing to do? At the moment it is 50/50. Like all schools, we will continue to 'do our duty', as we have been since March 23rd: educate our regulars in School, support home learning and manage our remote pastoral care system, plan for opening for more children and watch the national debate.

Rainbow poster by Elias

Monday 18th May
A number of the parents of our youngest children have been slow to respond to the offer of a School place. Perhaps, like the unions, they are waiting for more evidence that School will be safe before making a decision. At the moment it is looking like less than half of these year groups will return when the Government say it is safe to invite them back.

Spent the afternoon in a Zoom meeting with the Nursery, Reception and Year 1 teachers. Really helpful. The staff at North are brilliant. They have their worries and fears about having the youngest children back in School, but all their questions and suggestions were about making their rooms as safe as is possible. Conversations with other staff groups are planned through the week to build staff confidence and provide me with the detailed knowledge I need to complete the Risk Assessment.

Tuesday 19th May
The LA Risk Assessment pro forma leaves no aspect of school life unconsidered. 25 pages. Spent the day completing what I can. More conversations with the site manager, office staff, head of kitchen and support staff are required.

Wednesday 20th May
More councils around the country are saying the risk is too high to open schools to the priority year groups on June 1st, some citing that the infection rate and death rate is higher in their location. It makes sense to think like this. Knowing the local picture seems to be a better basis for decision making. After all, the R number could be lower than national which could actually boost confidence. It does not have to be a bad news story. This could be helpful to the Government because they still need to build confidence amongst parents and school staff. Last week I asked the Director of Education about the Essex R number. In my conference call with her and Union reps this morning she informed us that the R number for the East of England is 0.71. There is no figure for Essex. London's is currently 0.4.

Mrs. Shuter, the Head of Kitchen, is planning a menu for the little children with food that does not require a lot of cutting up because many of our four and five-year-olds still need help with this. She has also given thought to how the children can get their lunch without queuing at the servery. The kind of attention to detail that is required in these strange times.

Thursday 21st May
School will look and feel different. Parents know that.

This message was reinforced when the temporary school rules were emailed to them this morning along with a new Home School Accord. I wrote:

We are establishing rules to help everybody feel safe and be safe. If you do not feel that you and or your child can conform to these rules then you should reconsider your acceptance of the school offer. Similarly, if we feel that a parent or child's behaviour does not conform to the new rules then the offer may be withdrawn.

Some parents may find this alarming. The rules are a million miles away from the warm, welcoming community that is North. But whilst social distancing remains in force this is how we will run the School for the safety of everybody in it. So, some parents may actually find the stark and clear message reassuring.

Spent a lovely hour with Sonia Watson from BBC Essex. Sonia wanted to record a piece on school preparations for her breakfast radio show. We walked and talked. I showed her the yellow dots at 2m intervals which indicate where children and parents will wait outside the Nursery. I showed her what we are doing in the classrooms - creating workstations for 10 children where they will keep their belongings and have their own stationery set. Sharing and collaborating - the foundation of all happy, vibrant classrooms will have to be discouraged.

Nikki Greatorex from the Colchester Foodbank rang me. They will provide food vouchers for all our eligible families during Half-Term and the whole of the summer break. That is amazing. I told her I would be clapping for her too at 8.00pm.

Aimee helps to police the new rules in the playground

Friday 22nd May

Last day of the Half-Term. Today the whole School would normally be running round Hilly Fields to raise money for our Free For All campaign. The 24 children in School were allowed to wear their sporty clothes and did their running on the Astroturf. Our sports coach, Mrs. Eves, calculated that in total the children ran 43 miles – which if they had done it as a relay heading North East would have got the last child on to Aldeburgh beach!

The School Change Team convened for a Zoom meeting this morning. The School Change Team is a group that represents all the different staff and Union groups in the School. Two Governors sit on it too. It meets when the School is faced with a new challenge. The last time it convened was when we were going through a redundancy process due to underfunding. In previous years it has sat to discuss the School expansion to two-form entry in 2012. It enables all members of staff to feel they have a voice in major school affairs.

All staff groups are on board for welcoming our youngest pupils back. Over the holiday we will continue to prepare and we will wait for the PM's announcement which we are told will be made on the 28th. If June 1st is not the date, it may be June 8th or June 15th. Who knows, but we will be as ready as we can be.

Monday 25th is a Bank Holiday

The School is on its Half-Term break.

Tuesday 26th May

The School is closed for the first time since February 21st. But the cleaning team have been in School over the long weekend and today our Site Manager will complete the deep clean of the School ahead of the increasingly likely return of some of our youngest pupils next week. Some teachers have been in to start to prepare their 'bubbles' - a sparse learning environment for 10 pupils maximum. They will continue to come in through the week.

SES, an engineering company, start three months' work, upgrading the water supply, storage and heating system.

Sonia Watson did a good job on this morning's BBC Essex with her recorded piece on how we are preparing the School for the return of more pupils. Not sure who was listening though as there is only one topic of interest at the moment - the actions of Dominic Cummings, the PM's advisor. We teach our pupils from a very young age to take responsibility for their actions and to tell the truth at all times. And if they have done the wrong thing, accept the consequences and try to fix it if they can. I think Mr Cummings and his boss would have been spending some time in my office and asked to think very carefully about their actions.

Wednesday 27th May

With all the focus on Number 10, the announcement made yesterday by Junior Education Minister, Nick Gibb, to the select committee went unnoticed. There has been a change of mind on providing Free School Meal vouchers during this holiday week. Well, this is good news, but it will not help families in need this week and it will add to the School's administrative burden. Avoidable confusion.

This morning's conference call with the Local Authority discussed schools' risk assessments. The LA are still seeking clarity from the DfE on their guidance around suspected cases. This should have been provided weeks ago.

Spent the evening watching a crowdcast organised by the National Association of Headteachers, featuring a Q&A session with Dr Matt Butler, a Covid-19 specialist from Addenbrookes Hospital. He provided excellent practical advice on how to minimise risks in school. Really useful. He said the most important people in his hospital at the present time are not the doctors or nurses but the cleaners. He also said that in the absence of tests for under 5s we should treat all symptomatic three and four-year-olds as positive.

Thursday 28th May

5pm. The announcement is made. The PM says the five tests have been met. Schools should allow priority year groups back from June 1st. Other easing of lockdown measures were announced too. Sir Patrick Vallance, the Government's Chief Scientific Adviser, stressed caution. He says the R number is below one, but still high. Later in the evening it is reported that Sir David King, former Chief Scientific Adviser and Chair of the Independent Sage group, says with 8,000 new cases diagnosed every day, it is two weeks too soon to relax lockdown. Maybe coming out of lockdown will be harder than being in it. This situation lacks the certainty and simplicity of the stay at home message. Let us hope that this relaxation does not lead to over-exuberance which could trigger the fearful second wave.

Friday 29th May

Under 5s can now be tested. And the test and trace system was introduced nationally yesterday. This is important for many reasons. One of them being that the National Education Union says that schools should not admit more pupils until this system is in place. It crashed. Apparently, it is unlikely to be fully operational until the end of June.

Spent the day in School. The first hour I inspected the classrooms and playgrounds with the Site Manager. We are nearly there. We have sufficient supplies of cleaning products, paper towels and tissues and pedal bins. We also have gloves, aprons and masks in the event that intimate care or medical care is needing to be provided. This means that all bubbles can be fully independent.

Sent a memo to staff and Governors to keep them informed following the PM's announcement. Then prepared my briefing notes for my address to the staff who will be in School on Monday. I hope it is sunny because I will be briefing them in the open air, with them well spaced out. They will have the day - an INSET day - to complete their planning and finalise the logistical arrangements for their bubbles. Staff must remain loyal to their bubble, just like the children. Mixing is not allowed - a strict measure to avoid the virus spreading across the School. It makes sense but it is an incredibly inefficient use of staff and will make it impossible to take many more children if parental confidence does grow.

Staff and pupils must remain in their 'bubbles'

● North Primary School headteacher Alan Garnett gives his latest instalment of his pandemic diary, including on the decision to reopen our schools which is tied up in controversy

Tuesday, May 26
THE school is closed for the first time since February 21. However, the cleaning team have been in school over the long weekend and today our

■ Open again - North Primary School

Monday 1st June

In-Service Training (INSET) day. Last evening, I had planned to draft a letter to the parents who had accepted my offer to return their Nursery, Reception and Year 1 children to School tomorrow. The letter would have reminded them of the final arrangements. Staff have been working continually over the past three weeks, including through the holiday, to prepare for this event. They have been brilliant, as always, determined to do their best for the School.

Instead, I wrote a different letter. A letter informing parents that I will be deferring that decision until further notice.

I had said all along that I would re-open for the priority year groups when the Government said the five tests had been met. The PM made his announcement last Thursday that those five tests had indeed been met. He also announced a number of other measures to relax the lockdown. From Thursday evening onwards I became increasingly concerned as the PM's decision was questioned from a range of sources.

1. *The Government had admitted that we are still at Level 4. This was not made clear on Thursday. In fact, it came out that Professor Chris Whitty, the Chief Medical Officer for England, stopped the PM from downgrading the risk from Level 4 to Level 3.*

2. *The Independent SAGE group (led by a former Government Chief Scientific Advisor) feel that too much is being relaxed at the same time and recommended waiting until June 15th.*

3. *Last night senior Public Health officials, Association of Directors of Public Health, (ADPH), lobbied the Government to delay the easing of lockdown. The President of ADPH wrote: 'Now is the time for steady leadership, careful preparation and measured steps. The ADPH is calling for full implementation of all Phase 2 measures to be delayed until further consideration of the ongoing trends in infection rates and the R level gives more confidence about what the impact of these will be. There also must be a renewed drive to promote the importance of handwashing, social distancing and self-isolating if symptomatic, positive for COVID, or a contact of someone who is. And, additional assurance is required that the NHS Test and Trace System will be able to cope with the scale of the task.'*

In my letter I informed parents that as Headteacher of the School, with a duty of care to all the children and staff, I do not feel that the time has yet been reached where more children should be admitted back.

I am not a medical scientist, nor am I a politician. But I do feel like I am piggy in the middle. I feel that we should continue to be guided by the science and the science suggests we should remain cautious. Whilst we remain at Level 4, I would now rather wait to see what effect the relaxation of lockdown in society has on the R number and the infection rate.

I knew that parents who are trying to return to work would find my decision really unhelpful whilst others may simply disagree with my decision. But I did also consider that less than half of the parents had signed up for their children to return. Parental confidence is not yet there for most families. I invited parents to let me know their views.

Staff were briefed at 9.00am, in the open air, well spaced out across the Infant courtyard. I received a phone call from the Local Authority Standards and Excellent Partner (SEP) who needed to talk to me about my decision. A Microsoft Teams Meeting was scheduled for the afternoon.

Emails came in from parents through the day, all positive. These are typical:

You can't please everyone, but you can protect everyone. Of course we want to go back to work but things have to be right.

Two weeks ago we entertained the idea of possibly sending [our children] back to school. However we were not 100% over our original decision. Receiving your email this morning was most reassuring.

The conversation with my SEP lasted 100 minutes. He needed to provide a report to the Director of Education. He needed to establish that I had exercised due diligence.

In the evening I had a Zoom meeting with Governors. I was able to tell them that the LA would not be taking action against the School or Governors. There was overall backing from them for my decision and a strong commitment to support me but they rightly wanted to know what would happen next. I said we needed some time to see how things developed around the country and we agreed to meet again on the 11th. If the Scientists announce that the risk has gone down to Level 3, then I would let the youngest pupils back.

Tuesday 2nd June
Key Worker children returned to School, prepared for the new regime. Yellow dots, 2m apart everywhere. Adventure play equipment taped off. Parents had to sign the new Home School Accord, showing they and their children understood and would follow the new rules.

We have five Key Worker bubble groups with 10 children maximum in each and staff remaining faithful to their bubble and not mixing with other children and staff. This arrangement, one of the key requirements of the hierarchy of controls, completely limits staff distribution as each bubble has to be completely independent. No sending children to see the office staff for first aid. This must be done by the bubble staff only. MDAs (Midday Assistants) can't supervise the whole playground, just one bubble, with each bubble confined to a playground zone to prevent mixing. The staff: pupil ratio is excessive. All bubbles are equipped with cleaning products, new pedal bins, paper towels, PPE, first aid kits. They will keep their rooms spotless and the Site Manager will clean all toilets, light switches and door handles twice a day.

Everything will be thoroughly cleaned again by the cleaning team after School, every day.

Wednesday 3rd June
The views of the staff are that the new arrangements worked as we had hoped and the children coped well. Social distancing for young children is never going to be respected 100% of the time but the bubble system did limit those interactions.

Thursday 4th June
Teachers continue to manage the Home Learning systems and they and the support staff continue with the Keeping in Touch (KIT) phone calls. Incredibly time consuming but very worthwhile. Parental feedback from these calls remains appreciative of the home learning and KIT calls and supportive of my decision.

Friday 5th June
The NSA sent a letter to the Year 6s today. It was a lovely letter.

The last few months have been a strange and difficult time for so many people, but we think it's been particularly difficult for your year group. In any normal year, this would have been the time when you are working with your teachers and classmates to prepare for the transition to secondary school, as well as enjoying the various social activities that are organised to celebrate your achievements and wish you well in your next steps.

One of the things the NSA does is support the end of year bowling trip and meal for year 6s, which would typically take place in July. We want to make sure you don't miss out on this, which is why we have spoken to Mr. Garnett to confirm that we would like to support this, whenever it is safe to go ahead with it. This will hopefully be at some point in the Autumn, but we will monitor the situation and update you on proposed dates.

I would also like to take this opportunity to thank you for the tremendous contribution you have all made to the NSA events at North Primary over the years, and we look forward to welcoming you back as VIP alumni!

I am sure the children and their families will enjoy reading it.

Let us hope the weekend sees encouraging news from around the country and from the local area too.

Monday 8th June

Teachers sent home their weekly newsletters today. They are amazing. They showcase the work that the children are doing at home, not all of it set by the teachers, testament to the creativity of the children and the resourcefulness of their parents. Obviously I want all the children back at school and home learning has been a huge challenge for families, and we know that many children have not been engaged with their learning but we would be foolish to think that there are not positives to take from this experience when we return. Some of the ways of working and communicating, particularly the use of social media, where children are telling their teachers what is going well and what help they need to improve, should be built into the ways classrooms operate in the years ahead.

The weekend news was rightly dominated by the public rallies held around the country, triggered by the alleged murder of a black American citizen called George Floyd by a policeman. A girl in Year 5, unsolicited, sent a poster to her teacher.

I spent the afternoon speaking to our Home Learners of the Week. The children were animated about their learning and one was so proud to be nominated by his teacher that he cried.

All Lives Matter, by Joey

Tuesday 9th June

The Secretary of State made a speech in the House of Commons today. He announced that most children would not be back in School before September. Saddened that this is being portrayed by some as due to the resistance of school leaders and teachers to having more children back. Whilst schools have to respect social distancing rules it was always a logistical impossibility. The Secretary got attacked by all parties for not having recovery plans in place. 'Kids can go to theme parks but not school' sums up the confused picture of life as we leave lockdown. Unfortunately debate in the House of Commons is reduced to a lot of knee-jerk point-scoring from all parties. When any Government is on the defensive, bad policy follows. Education never fares well when it is used as a political football.

Wednesday 10th June

Here we go. Plans for Summer catch-up are now being drawn up, even though there is real doubt over all children returning to School in September. So then we will have Christmas Catch-up and so it will go on. Is there nobody in the DfE who can look at the bigger picture, do a proper analysis and come up with a long-term vision that might even build something better than what we had before?

Sent off emails to the NAHT, Gavin Williamson, the Education spokespersons for the Labour Party and the Liberal Democrats with a proposal for education recovery. Here goes:

Reception, Year 1, Year 2, Year 3, Year 4, Year 5, Year 7, Year 8, Year 9, Year 10, Year 12 repeat a year. This will cost the Government nothing this year and will build in additional time for pupils to 'catch up' if we are not all back full-time from September.

Year 6 and Year 11 move on as per usual, but there should be significant additional investment for these two cohorts to provide appropriate support - based on identified need - pastoral as well as academic.

This leaves one pressure point in the system - the children who would be starting school in September - the rising fives. There will be no room for them. Now, they have missed out on important early years experiences and the start of their school careers will not be how we would want it. So they would remain pre-schoolers. This will put pressure on pre-school provision as the under 4s scrabble for places not vacated by the rising 5s. And this is where the investment should go, seizing the opportunity to do things better.

Private Nursery provision has been decimated by the pandemic. State Nursery provision has been underfunded for some years now. Rather than throw money at some ill-thought out catch-up programmes, there should be a massive injection into pre-school provision. This would not only save the sector, which is currently at risk of going under, but enable it to be expanded and address the disadvantage gap through universal provision before children start school. Children would then start school a year later, bringing us closer in line with the best models from around the world.

There would be issues to address around school age, exam years etc, but these are insignificant compared to what we can best do to find the best route out of the present crisis.

Time for a lie down!

Thursday 11th June

Meanwhile, we continue to prepare for September and letters have gone out to families of children starting Nursery and Reception in September.

Prepare for this evening's Governors meeting. Do I now invite Nursery, Reception and Year 1 children back to School? I informed parents that I would do that when we moved to Covid Alert Level 3. Unfortunately basing my decision on the alert level has hit a problem. On May 10th, the PM said the pandemic alert level would be categorised on a scale of one to five in different parts of the country, based on assessments by a new 'joint biosecurity centre', (JBC). This centre has not been established yet. It has appointed a Chair, Claire Gardiner, but Health Secretary Matt Hancock admitted that it still 'formally needs to come into existence.' Tom Hurd, who was the temporary Head of the unit, had said, '*The JBC is expected to reach full operating capacity later in the summer.*' Really helpful.

In other words, I will be waiting a very long time for the JBC to make a decision. I can't wait for that. So, I made my decision based on the following: the decline in new infection rates in the region; the positive experience of other schools; the success of the key worker bubbles in North; and our own risk assessment which has clear guidance on procedures for managing suspected and confirmed cases of Covid-19. The Governors support my decision to bring those children back to school - if their parents want it - for the last month of the Summer Term.

Friday 12th June

Informed the whole School community of my decision. Had a lovely phone conversation with a granddad who has been helping his grandson with his maths, remotely, of course - they have not been able to see each other since March. Maths is not taught like how it was to him in the Fifties! He asked when School re-opens could he watch some maths lessons so that he can carry on helping his grandson. We had a lovely chat. What a nice way to finish the week.

Monday 15th June

Further to my announcement that our youngest pupils could return to School from the 22nd there was not a great deal of new interest shown by parents so the take-up remains under 50%. The DfE missed another deadline last Friday - they said schools would be informed by the 12th how they could interpret flexibility to accommodate other year groups before the end of Term. The Local Authority were told today by the DfE that they did not know when this information would be published.

Tuesday 16th June

Oh, breaking news, flexibility will be defined by the Government today, after all. And having read it there is actually not a lot of wriggle room - no using village halls as classrooms, no spending extra money on staff, must maintain the full-time offer to the priority year groups and key worker children. This news is overshadowed by a Government U-turn on providing food vouchers for families eligible for Free School Meals over the Summer Holiday. Take a bow Marcus Rashford. The first time I have ever praised a Manchester United player. His letter to the PM has seemingly struck a chord with a number of Conservative MPs and before the matter could be debated in the House of Commons the announcement was made.

Spent the afternoon in a conference call with Councillor Ray Gooding, Chair of the Essex Education Committee, Local Authority officials and Union representatives. Cllr Gooding said that teachers had had their Easter Holiday taken from them, the LA would not be taking their Summer Holiday. There is a clear understanding within the LA that there is no short-term fix for pupils and schools need to focus their energies on planning for the Autumn Term and beyond, whilst all too aware of the uncertainties around the next Academic Year.

Wednesday 17th June

I added to my teachers' workload by asking them to complete a form auditing their workload. The professionalism of the staff is remarkable. As if I did not know that. The number of posts - work and comments made by children and their parents - they are responding to every week; the videos and learning tasks they are setting, the time spent making the keeping in touch phone calls. Staggering.

Thursday 18th June

A quiet day, just an announcement about an announcement - the Government's plans for catch-up would be published soon. My proposal for education recovery has been met with a deafening silence - not even an acknowledgement. I now realise that I sent it to the wrong people. I assumed that sending it to Ministers, politicians and the Children's Commissioner was the right thing to do. Silly me. I should have sent it to a Premier League footballer and asked him to promote it. Harry Kane says *children and young people deserve a world beating education recovery plan!* Obvious Headline – PM given the Kane!

Friday 19th June

On the way to work I listen to Nick Gibb, Schools' Minister, publicising the Government's billion-pound recovery plan. A massive amount of money - spread over two years and requiring funding contribution from schools. The plan lacks detail but he suggests some scope will be given to schools on how it will be spent on tutoring programmes. The Minister comes unstuck when he is asked to explain his assertion that all children will be back in School full-time from September.

I did say to parents that I would not let the youngest return to School until we move to threat Level 3. Well, this morning that announcement was made, but the scientists were quick to emphasise the need to not change our behaviours. This point was reinforced in the most honest and sobering way by Mike Gogarty, Director of Wellbeing, Public Health and Communities. Mike is employed by ECC but his role is independent and he was invited by the Director of Education, Clare Kershaw, to attend a conference call following a letter I wrote asking what a local response to an outbreak will look like.

Mike's message was stark: lockdown is the only measure that has worked so far; social distancing is required until a vaccine is found; the distance may reduce and there are economic and political influences on this decision but he is clear on the medical science position that social distancing should remain; it is impossible to open all schools full-time and keep the R number below 1; and there will be a Winter spike and lockdowns will be necessary. So, what did he think could/should happen if/when there is an outbreak in Essex?

Firstly, if there was a local outbreak in an institution like a hospital or school or college then that would be fairly easy to shut and isolate because those organisations would comply, he said. But if there was an outbreak in a commercial area that would be tricky because businesses would be reluctant to close. He said that he would need to explore his powers which would involve liaison with the Police Commissioner. And if an outbreak was more widespread across a locality, then central Government would be involved.

At tea-time Secretary of State, Gavin Williamson, reinforced the message that schools will be back full-time in September. How we would all love that. But how does this fit with the medical science message? I suppose we all open in the knowledge that at some point we will have to shut when we get the Winter spikes. How we need a vaccine.

Must end the week on a positive. Send a video to all the staff and Governors. A sneak preview of the film of a day in the life of our 60 Reception children. It was made by local filmmakers Cliqq Studio. Wow, what a job they have done. It captures perfectly the vibrancy and variety of our five-year-olds school day... at a time before lockdown, before social distancing and 'hierarchies of control' risk reduction measures. A time when school was buzzy and spontaneous. So a happy film but sadly poignant too.

First day back: Year 1 bubble lining up

Monday 22nd June

First day back for Nursery, Reception and Year 1. That is seven bubbles in total. Everything seemed to go to plan. The staggered timings worked; Home School Accords were signed and handed in; the one-way system on and off the site worked, and the yellow dots on the playground to indicate where to line up worked. The parents behaved impeccably - well nearly all! A couple had to sit on the naughty step for minor misdemeanour's. Most importantly, the children soon settled into their bubbles. One little girl, Doris, had the thrill of returning to School on her 6th birthday. The bubbles are set up, following the Government guidance to enable social distancing to happen

Doris returns to school on her birthday

but children cannot keep to that every minute and there are many other risk minimising measures in place: staff not mixing, ventilation, outdoor activities, limiting resources, regular hand washing, regular cleaning of surfaces, fresh clothing every day, and parents and staff know that swift action would be taken if someone is symptomatic. I thanked the staff for adapting to their new working environment and doing a fantastic job, as they always do.

Tuesday 23rd June

This morning I had a telephone interview with an HMI seconded to the Local Authority. He was asking me about my plans for September. I told him I am in the process of consulting with senior leaders about this ahead of a teacher meeting tomorrow. I told him the same as I wrote to parents yesterday:

The Government is saying that all children will be back full-time. This would be lovely but is a logistical impossibility under the current arrangements. We are waiting for the guidance on how this can be achieved. You may or may not be surprised to know that Headteachers do not get told of the Government's plans before you do. And given the uncertainty of Covid the guidance may change in August. In the meantime, we are planning for the bit that we can control—putting the interests of your children first. You will receive more detailed information soon.

Watched the PM lead the daily briefing - the last one - at 5pm. He announced a range of measures easing lockdown and repeated the pledge that all schools would have all children in school in September in bubbles of 30. Still no detail as to how that can happen. At least in primary, children are generally taught in the same classroom by the same teacher. Secondary schools face far bigger challenges. Maybe the students will do a week of one subject with one teacher and then the school is deep cleaned over the weekend and the children are taught a different subject the following week.

Wednesday 24th June

I do love holding remote meetings. I can put everybody on mute! Teacher meeting after school. I shared my thinking about the organisation for September, basing my plans on what we know: some children have done lots of work and made good use of their time; some children have not and may be completely out of routine; some may struggle to return and all may struggle with stamina – they will not be match fit for five days full on, but children are amazingly resilient so returning to a place where they feel secure and get to see their friends will enable them to settle quickly. We also know that Covid-19 is not going away.

What we don't know is: what the guidance will be regarding the school offer in September; which children are going to struggle upon their return and we will not make assumptions about that; and what the gaps are in their learning and we will not make assumptions about that either.

So, in September, as much as is possible, we want the children to return to a School they are familiar with – same classroom, same staff who they know well and know them best. I hear worrying things that schools are talking of getting the children to sit tests as soon as they return and then cramming them so they 'catch up'. This will not be the approach at North. The Broad and Balanced Curriculum is sacrosanct - we will not punish the children for being isolated at home in lockdown. We are not testing and cramming. And the research backs this up. The evidence from countries where their school system shut down for several months - like in New Zealand after their earthquake in 2011 - is really helpful and should be used to help with our planning.

In September the children will start off where they left off and, once their teachers have got them back into the routine and we have a clear understanding of their emotional health and where they are with their learning, they will then transition into their new classes. How long this will take will be determined by the Government guidance on school opening. Hopefully no more than two to three weeks.

This plan is well received by the teachers.

Oh my goodness, get home, sit in the garden and read the Government's updated guidance: the DfE has re-written history. 'Primary pupils do not and have not needed to be kept apart in the classroom' This is blatantly untrue and is quickly proven to be so on social media and print media - showing the wording in the original guidance. Seemingly the DfE are implying, the measures put in place have not all been necessary. The DfE is actually gaslighting schools – trying to blame us for the low numbers of children in schools. This won't do and it will undermine their efforts to get every child back. They still need to build parental confidence and reassure staff too. They won't achieve this by behaving dishonestly.

Harrison, Izzy and Jacob, Year 1 pupils, in their socially distanced classroom

Reception children spread out eating their lunch - table for 1

Thursday 25th June
Finally some sensible news coming out of the DfE. The new national Baseline assessment system to be introduced for our rising fives starting in September has been put on hold. These children were to have been the first cohort to have their progress measured from the start of primary to the end of primary, meaning there would be no statutory assessment for them at the end of KS1. With so much uncertainty this is a sensible, pragmatic decision. I wonder if they will make similar announcements about phonics tests, Year 4 table tests and the Year 6 SATs tests.

Friday 26th June
The week ended as it started - advising parents on how they can monitor, advise and guide their children in their use of social media. Of course, the advice concerns their own children's misuse and how to deal with the misuse by others. The technology has been so helpful over the past few months but it can expose children to harm and exploit their vulnerabilities. It is vital that children feel that they can talk to their parents about these matters and that parents parent.

Farewells at the end of a testing year

● North Primary School head Alan Garnett reflects on a challenging term

■ Homely - Colchester's North Primary School

weeks. The document does not mention the wearing of face masks as standard practice, only when managing intimate care or supervising

new to headship. How tough must it have been for them?

What has become clear to me over the past few months is that, paradoxically,

Monday 29th June

Parents were informed today of the plans to start the new Academic Year two days earlier with the children returning to their familiar classrooms and teaching teams that they know. I have asked for the parents of our new starters (the rising fives) and our current Reception cohort to bear with us as they will have a more gradual start to the year. Feedback is positive so far: *'It has clearly taken a lot of thought from all the staff and that effort does not go unnoticed.'*

Had a visit from a Police Community Support Officer (PCSO) this morning who introduced himself as our link officer. The Police are looking to re-establish community links with schools. This has to be a good move for any number of reasons. Years ago, this relationship was about building trust and being a visible presence in the area. Sadly, there is another more sinister menace driving this current initiative - the recruitment of younger children into county lines drug gangs.

Monday afternoon routine of ringing our Home Learners of the Week is always a pleasure. Not only is it nice to talk to the children, it is also nice to have a quick chat with the parents too, especially as I don't get to see many of them in the playground at the moment. One mum told me that she has enjoyed learning more about her daughter's work, giving her a greater understanding of what we do and how her daughter is learning. Other parents were singing the praises of the teachers for their creativity and constant support. Good to hear.

Tuesday 30th June

Said goodbye to a teacher this week who has been covering for a maternity leave. It will be a shame that he will not be able to say goodbye to his class in person, likewise for the children and parents. No assembly send-off either. In all, three teachers are returning from maternity leave in the coming week. It will be good to welcome them back. They might notice School is a little different since they were last in!

Wednesday 1st July

Informed parents today that only children leaving the School and Nursery this Term will be receiving annual reports: they are our Year 6 leavers and Nursery children who are going to another school. For the rest of the children a report would be lacking information – no end of year assessment, no annual attendance data - and so a report written in June, and read by parents in July, about children who have not been in School since March would not be a particularly relevant document. Children and parents have been better served by the teachers' time and focus concentrating on managing home learning and the keeping in touch calls. Paradoxically, this has meant that for many, the communication and information sharing between home and school has been more regular than in pre-Covid times.

Thursday 2nd July

It has been published. The much-heralded document providing 35 pages of guidance on how we can have all our children back in school full-time in September.

The focus in the Press has been on the logistics. My eye is drawn to the guidance on responding to a suspected or confirmed case. At the present time we are sending bubbles home if a child or adult in that bubble is a confirmed case, and they all isolate for 14 days. If someone is symptomatic the same action is taken until a test is taken and the result received. These are autonomous decisions, driven by the risk assessment to coin the phrase. This course of action is reassuring to parents and staff.

From September the guidance says that we should not send the rest of the bubble home if there is a suspected case, and if there is a confirmed case, we seek advice from the local health protection team who may then direct certain people to be sent home. I was comfortable with a full return if we would still be acting swiftly in our own institutions to 'whack the mole', as the PM likes to call the local response strategy. I think parental confidence would be higher too, which is vital if we are to get all the children back. The guidance also states we should not ask a parent to confirm a negative test result. I am struggling to understand why that is in the document, especially as the guidance states that we all need to engage with test and trace. Sent an email to the Director of Public Health Essex for his thoughts.

Friday 3rd July

Read the guidance for the third time. Now focussing on the logistical challenges of 420 schoolchildren and 30 nursery children having staggered starts, playtimes, lunchtimes and home times and of course, inbetween those events, educating the children. The guidance says we must *'minimise contacts while delivering a broad and balanced curriculum'* whose key principles are *'broad and ambitious'* whilst *'creating time to cover the most important missed content'* so we *'may consider it appropriate to suspend some subjects.'* Total clarity! The Government is seeing criticism of its document, which is confused and contradictory and driven by expediency rather than medical science, as obstructive and negative. I disagree. Schools and local authorities are just trying to make sense of the guidance and make it work. In the final section of the document it says,

The people who do the work are often the best people to understand the risks in the workplace and will have a view how to work safely. Involving them in making decisions shows that the school takes their H&S seriously.

A statement I can agree with. This sentiment works equally well if the word school is replaced with Government.

Monday 6th July

Must get on with the plan for return of all 450 children in September. Before getting bogged down with the logistics I need to know what the LA's view is on the very different response schools will make to suspected and confirmed Covid cases. In my conference call this morning Clare Kershaw said that she feels there are factors and measures which make this new response proportionate. She announced that Essex has now got a Health Protection Board. Mike Gogarty, Director of Public Health and Wellbeing for Essex, chairs, and she is a member. They meet weekly on a Monday and sat for the first time last week. The Board get Covid test information at postcode level and will get local testing data which relates to schools and businesses. This is encouraging. Essex has produced an Outbreak Control Plan which has been approved by the NHS. I have asked for this document to be placed in the public domain. So we must trust that by September the slowly improving test and trace system, the speed with which results are returned and with the Public Health Board getting relevant data quickly, and with schools continuing to adhere to the hierarchy of controls, we will have in place a strong enough system to limit the infection rate and also manage and contain outbreaks.

Microsoft Teams meeting with the senior management team this afternoon. An hour spent talking about bubbles. Who would have thought! There is agreement that we have a workable structure but there are so many details to address to implement the plan effectively.

Tuesday 7th July

We are not the only people working hard on our plans. Received an email from Mike Gogarty this morning in which he signed off, *'What we are all clear on is that there is much work we need to do well before September to define best approach and we are committed to do this.'*

Wednesday 8th July

Our Year 6's should be busy rehearsing their play - a fabulous way to end their primary careers. They are having to settle for compiling a video and staff are putting together a video too as there will not be a Leavers' Assembly. I recorded my message. Very strange feeling. It is hard to maintain that sense of community when everybody - even those within the School - are isolated and deliberately being kept apart.

Community is about belonging and giving, and North is lucky to have so many people from our locality who want to make a contribution to our School. We are privileged to have benefited from employees of local businesses Hiscox, and more recently Seatrade, who give up their lunchtimes to pop into School and support the children with their learning and read with them. Some of the volunteers have been doing this for years – others stopped because they decided they wanted a career change and went off to train to become teachers. Well, visitors are not currently welcome in schools. Out of the blue we received an email from two of our volunteers who have been helping out in the Year 6 classrooms up until lockdown. *'When we could visit you, it was an absolute pleasure to be welcomed into your classes and to spend a small amount of time each week in your wonderful company. It's a shame that we couldn't come in to see you before you go to make you next big step into secondary school, however we wish you all the best in your new schools, with your new uniforms and the new friends you are about to make.'* A lovely gesture. The teachers will pass on this message.

Thursday 9th July

The day starts with another meeting with senior managers who have been emailing their thoughts and ideas, and ends with an evening Full Governing Body Zoom meeting. What will School look like? No singing, no playing woodwind instruments, PE without physical contact, no assemblies, dining rooms not practical to be used, staggered starts with playground drop zones to help segregate parents with children in different bubbles. Another challenge will be to have a full remote learning offer available throughout the year whilst the School is fully operational. A massive undertaking. Governors ask about the Government's catch-up scheme. I inform them that there are no details yet on how to access the grants and what we can and can't spend them on. Nine school days left. August will be busy.

The New School Year normally starts with all staff and Governors - over 70 people - gathering to hear me set out the vision for the year. I also give a safeguarding briefing, ensuring all staff and Governors are up to speed with the latest guidance - usually published in the holiday for implementation from September 1st. Governors approve the plans and also rubber stamp the extensive programme of Summer works which will include the major repair of the crumbling ceiling in the music studio, which is currently unsafe to use.

Friday 10th July

Excellent news. The LA capital programme team confirm they will pay for the new ceiling in the music studio. That will save the School over £10,000. We lose control of the project but that is a price worth paying as they say they can match our timescales and get the work completed in the holiday.

This afternoon, met with Laura Davison, co-ordinator for CXXV, our 125th birthday history project. There cannot be many Schools in the country who have chronicled in such detail the living history of their school and the community which they serve. The high-profile events and lessons which got the year off to such an incredible start back in November seem a memory from a distant time but there is still plenty of work that needs to be done: complete the archive, upload all the oral histories and artefacts onto the website timeline, and get the history book finished and off to the printers. In a normal world we would be looking to hold a big event in November to bring the birthday year to a fitting conclusion with the book launch but who knows if indoor social gatherings will be allowed even then?

Monday 13th July

Parents are children's first and therefore their most important teachers. In our Nursery we take the children and expand their knowledge, teach them new skills and broaden their understanding of the world around them. In a phrase, the children in Nursery learn how to learn - with and alongside others. Today we posted annual reports to children in the Nursery who will be attending a different school in September. Those reports are such fun to read – capturing the children's enjoyment of learning through play. I hope those reports are read and stored somewhere so that when the children are much older, they can take it out of their 'special box' and look back with fondness on their learning journey in Nursery. Year 6s had their reports posted too. Their reports are very different this year and certainly provide a fascinating contrast with the Nursery reports. This year the teachers have written the report as a letter with this introduction -

North Primary has been a vital part of your learning and I hope that you can take the time to think about all the valuable experiences that you have had and reflect on your time here. Although we have not been able to celebrate the end of your period at North in the usual ways, it is important that you celebrate your achievements over the last year, and previous years, so that you can feel confident that you are ready for the next stage of your life. Our beautiful school has been a stimulating and happy place for you to learn and the values that you have lived by during your time here will provide you with the belief that you can achieve anything you want to at secondary school.

The reports then go on to provide advice on how each child can make that happen. Very moving, most definitely reports to treasure.

Tuesday 14th July

Zoom School Change Team meeting today. Representatives from all parts of the School sit on this group. It is the perfect vehicle for consultation. They know their roles inside out and provide great insight and ask really important questions. They are in broad agreement that we have a viable plan for September; it is going to be very challenging and they have identified plenty of creases that need ironing out. But yes, we do have a workable plan if we increase our staffing capacity around lunchtimes, which will cost money. The DfE has said there will be no additional money made available to enable schools to open fully. Had a Zoom meeting this evening with Heads from around the county – All members of the NAHT. Unanimous agreement on essential additional staffing costs. Expenditure on hand hygiene is huge too. Some schools have also lost money because the DfE changed the rules earlier in lockdown and backtracked on promises to reimburse schools for certain additional costs. So schools that went out of their way to make sure their most vulnerable children did not go hungry are significantly out of pocket. How is that OK?

Wednesday 15th July

Not only do we need more staff over lunchtimes because of the need to avoid large numbers eating together and using the playground, there is no slack in the system if we have staff absence. Emails go out making sure staff register their other jobs – the last thing we want is for Covid to be brought into the School from other places of work - or vice versa. I also need to have individual meetings with staff who are in vulnerable groups. They all need to have confidence in the plans.

Thursday 16th July

Read the Essex County Council's Outbreak Control Plan this morning. It is incredibly detailed and gives confidence that there will be a strong and swift response to local outbreaks come September. But the plan illustrates how precarious the situation is – there are so many reasons why children and staff may not be able to come to School - for up to 14 days at a time if they have to self-isolate. I think there will be occasions when a class will not be able to open because of staff unavailability. Apparently two schools in the East of England have been shut recently because their kitchen staff tested positive. As I say, the situation is precarious.

Friday 17th July

The final Friday of the Term. Tradition has it that we hold an Open Evening - an opportunity for families to tour the School, look at all the work on display and in books, say goodbyes and thank yous to the children's current teachers and meet the children's next teachers. The School is full, it always looks magnificent, and there is a wonderful atmosphere. Not this year.

The staff have made a film for Year 6. They will get it next week. I had a preview this morning. Staff share their memories of the group, all the way back to Nursery where many of them started. It is lovely. The children will like it. It is a fitting tribute to their primary school careers, spanning up to eight years. It is also a testament to the brilliance of the staff at North. This will form a perfect companion piece for the film the children themselves have made. With contributions made in their own homes, edited by an older brother, the children have managed to record a song. The film manages to capture the children's personalities. It is warm and funny. Lots of happy tears will flow watching these films.

Monday 20th July

There is something about North that makes it hard to leave. I am only its eighth headteacher. Teachers have collectively dedicated about 200 years of their careers to the School and Nursery. And the same can be said of the Governors. Our Chair of Governors, Jan Blackwell, appointed me in 2000. In total, she has clocked up 30 years of voluntary service to the school community. Jan is a dentist but she has set aside every Wednesday morning over those years to spend time in the School, checking I am on top of everything and helping out in the Reception classes, meaning that she has got to know all the children who start the School as rising fives. Remarkable. She sent an email to all the staff today. Here is part of it:

Jan Blackwell, Chair of Governors, presenting a petition for the school funding campaign to local MP Will Quince in 2019.

We started the school year looking forward to celebrating our 125th birthday. Who could have predicted that we would be catapulted into the 21 Century with online learning as the norm.

On behalf of the Governors, I would like to thank you all for stepping up to the challenge, not only of teaching in a very different way, but interacting with the families through Keeping in Touch calls and safeguarding, as best possible, the welfare of the children.

She has also written a letter to parents which I will include in my final newsletter of the year.

Tuesday 21st July

Today I finally finish the Risk Assessment for September. The key section outlines the procedures to be followed if staff or children have symptoms or test positive. There is a clear anomaly in the Government guidance. If a child tests positive they have to isolate for seven days; the other members of the household have to self-isolate for 14 days. So how does the young child get to school from days 8-14? Have I been reading all these documents for too long? Check with LA Communication Team that I have understood this instruction correctly. Yes, I have.

The Risk Assessment will be shared with staff and put on the website and will be under constant review. And a lot can change over the next six weeks. The document does not mention the wearing of face masks as standard practice, only when managing intimate care or supervising a symptomatic child whilst waiting for the parent to come and take them home. From Friday it will be compulsory in all shops. Possibly by September there will be similar advice for schools. By sheer coincidence I receive two emails from parents on this subject. Their views could not be further apart. One asks that I make the wearing of face masks compulsory for all children and staff in September. The other from a health care professional, urges me to resist such a plan, citing evidence that the wearing of masks is not effective and can be counter-productive.

The PM announced pay rises for public sector workers. Good news for teachers but where will the money come from to pay them? All indications are that the money will have to come from within our existing budget. Two years ago Learning Support Assistants got a well-deserved pay rise, Schools ended up making some LSAs redundant so they could afford to honour the pay rises for the rest.

The Year 6s got sent their song video and the 35 minute long video message from staff. It was very well received as this email from a parent indicates:

Wow. Thank you for such a beautiful goodbye video for the Year 6's. I was literally sobbing. [My daughter] and I really appreciate how much thought and effort went into it. The goodbye messages, memories and wishes for the future were heartfelt and amazing. The end of primary school didn't quite go to plan, but we do have some amazing memories of the past 7 years, an excellent education, and some lifelong friendships.

Wednesday 22nd July
The final day of the Academic Year has arrived. To say it has been a challenge is an understatement. I feel for colleagues in other schools new to headship. How tough must it have been for them?

What has become clear to me over the past few months is that, paradoxically, for many parents, remote learning has brought home and school closer together. So in my final Newsline I shared a letter from a parent who captured that sentiment perfectly.

We just wanted to write to you to say how thankful we are for all that you have done for the children during this bizarre time.

The teachers have set sufficient work which has always been marked or commented on and sent back for corrections, kept in touch and has never put any pressure on us parents or children to get work done. It has always been about their wellbeing for which we are very grateful and they did all this while looking after and teaching their own children!

We are so appreciative of the information and support that has been given to us from all members of staff and that the children's health and wellbeing, as well as the staff, are the priority.

In September, we are so pleased with how you are planning to proceed. We have an anxious child, as I'm sure you're aware, and by allowing him to settle back into school with familiar teachers is a big help and is very reassuring for him.

Normally, we would've given to teachers a gift at this time of year but I'm sure the best gift you all could have is some time off!

The final afternoon. Year 6's pop in for an hour to collect their belongings left in classrooms and cloakrooms since March 23rd; a memory stick with their year book, their leavers' hoodies and a gift from Eld Lane Church. For a number of years now Susan Sydenham visits the Year 6's and talks to them about their journey from primary to secondary and presents them with a very good book about preparing for that transition.

The children are sat spaced out on the Astroturf in the fresh air and sunshine, socially distancing but they have not seen each other for a long time so that is harder for some than others. It is lovely to see them. A very kind grandparent has paid for a freelance photographer to capture these moments. For 27 of the children this is also the end of their parents' connection with the school as these children are either their only or youngest. The parents have to say their farewells at the school gate. One day they may return as grandparents. It is hard to stay away from North forever. It is that kind of school.

Year 6 leavers hoodie

Year 6's return to School to collect their belongings and meet their friends. For many, it was, the first time they had returned to school since the lockdown in March. 6A above, 6S below. Images by Seana Hughes.

Rainbow of hope, by pupils in 5S

■ Welcome back - Colchester's North Primary School

Changing face of school life

Tuesday, September 1

THE final day of the summer holiday. The Bank Holiday weather suggested we are going to skip September and head straight for October.

The exam fiasco seems to have preoccupied everybody in the DfE because it issues new guidance for schools late on Friday night – twice! Fortunately, it does not require me to alter the information I have shared with parents.

■ In his regular Gazette diary, North Primary School headteacher Alan Garnett reflects on an unusual start to the new autumn term

rent regulations.

At 8.25am I open the gates at the back of the school. There are some very happy, and relieved, parents, and lots of very smart and smiley children. The one-way system and the staggered start times work pretty well.

North is a wonderfully diverse community school. Assemblies are a time when we can create and foster that sense of belonging and pride

Tuesday 1st September

The final day of the Summer Holiday. The Bank Holiday weather suggested we are going to skip September and head straight for October. The GCSE and A Level exam fiasco seems to have preoccupied everybody in the DfE because it issues new guidance for schools late on Friday night – twice! Fortunately it does not require me to alter the information I have shared with parents. They have been told of the new arrangements - first year group to arrive at 8.30 via Victoria Chase, one parent only hopefully who must then leave via John Harper Street. They also know exactly what must happen if someone is symptomatic or tests positive. Hopefully they have prepared their children for how different School will be. Parents have also been reminded to inform the School if their children are in quarantine, and when will be the first day that they can return to school. We have only one member of staff in quarantine and just until the weekend.

Lots of children will be starting at the School having moved in to the area. They are given tours of the School. Not so straightforward. Making sure everybody social distances and avoids the contractors that are everywhere.

It has been an unbelievably busy six weeks. A new ceiling has been fitted in one of the classrooms; a new plumbing system runs through the school, feeding off the new water supply and heated by a brand new boiler fitted in the cellar; classrooms decorated, deep cleans everywhere, carpentry repairs, grounds work. Sadly, the Music Studio will not be ready - it needs a new ceiling and that will be completed next week. Worst of all, a beautiful, mature, silver birch tree has to come down. That will take today and tomorrow. We look a long way from being ready to welcome all the children back.

Wednesday 2nd September

A training day. This is the day when all the staff gather - kitchen, office, lunchtime - everybody, with the Governors - in the Junior Hall and I present the plans for the year ahead. Not this year. Staff are scattered around the School, Governors are at home and I Zoom my presentations. No communal coffee breaks or lunch.

Last year's School Improvement Plan has been dusted off as it was not possible to action most of it, instead we have a School Recovery Plan which is shared along with the key elements of the Covid-19 Risk Assessment. I also give the staff and Governors a safeguarding briefing. The DfE update their Keeping Children Safe in Education document, which schools have to implement from September 1st. It was published on August 31st! This timescale is the same every year.

There are too many people Zooming to make these sessions interactive. I am just a talking head. Staff will email their questions, concerns and suggestions. They spend the rest of the day preparing to welcome their old class back tomorrow. The midday team are spaced out around the Infant Hall for a briefing. Staggered lunch breaks will be introduced and they will have a class each to supervise eating their lunch in their classrooms and then playing in class playground zones. The midday staff will also clean the classroom surfaces and toilets.

The Site Manager informs me that the extractor fan in the kitchen, which is linked to the gas supply, has just failed. An electrician will come at 6.30 in the morning to fix it.

Thursday 3rd September

Bad news – not able to cook hot meals in the kitchen. The extractor fan is 30 years old and does not comply with current regulations. Email sent to parents to inform them that it will be a pack-up service for the rest of the week. Essex County Council is informed.

At 8.25am I open the gates at the back of the School. There are some very happy, and relieved, parents, and lots of very smart and smiley children. The one-way system and the staggered start times work pretty well. Just a few tweaks required. North is a wonderfully diverse community school. Assemblies are a time when we can create and foster that sense of belonging and pride.

At 9.40am I lead the whole School Assembly from my office talking into my laptop on Zoom. The children are sat in their classrooms. Strange. I welcome them all, they say hello and then the teachers press their mute buttons. At the end of the assembly, they are unmuted and all the classes come on screen and they can all see each other waving. A nice moment. So that is what community will look like now.

Meeting with our music teacher. Music is very high profile at North. Every child gets the opportunity to be taught to play at least three instruments, free of charge. He talks me through what can and can't happen. The Government guidance will make it difficult to have our saxophone, flute and clarinet lessons. He reassures me that these lessons can go ahead. 'You can't blow out a candle with a trombone,' he says. There will be mitigations but these instruments can be played. It is sound waves that come out the end of these instruments, not spittle. Obvious really.

Recorders are a different matter. Our Year 3's will not be given recorders this year. The rest of the day goes well. Parents had been sent an email informing them of the adjustments to the pick-up regime. Teacher meeting to review the day. Teachers dotted around the hall. Lots of what went wells and a few even better ifs. Another email goes out to parents.

Attendance was very good. Only a handful of non-Covid absences, a few quarantine/travel issues. Just two families have decided to home educate their children because of their concerns about school safety.

Friday 4th September
Parents stop on arrival, to tell me how pleased they are with how the School is managing the new normal. Good to hear.

Assembly does not go to plan. A member of staff knocks on my door to tell me that they can't connect. Nobody has, apparently. I have been talking to myself for a few minutes. Embarrassing. Reschedule for later in the day.

The kitchen saga takes a turn for the worse. The County will not pay for the kitchen work - estimates are in the region of £20,000. Inform parents that the kitchen will not be cooking hot meals for a few weeks.

Paper chains by Year 5. The children are pleased to be back in school.

Monday 7th September 2020

Today should have been the day that our oldest year group travelled to Dorset for a week of outdoor adventures. Not this year. The trip has been moved to April. Let's hope that it can happen then.

At the other end of the School, our Early Years teams welcome the four-year-olds for their first taste of school life. Smart uniforms, big eyes beaming nervous excitement. Magic moments.

The weekly comms email from the LA includes an attachment which has suggested wordings to reply to parents who are challenging School Covid procedures. A small but vocal social media group are basically Covid deniers, making life difficult for some schools. One of the issues this group has is they do not want their children isolated in school if they become symptomatic. Well, the policy is isolate and send home to get tested. Non-negotiable. Same rules for staff. How else can we contain the virus and keep our schools open?

A parent - a health professional - caught me by surprise at the School gate this morning. She asked what provision the School has in place to look after key worker children in the event that they become symptomatic in School? Apparently she and other healthcare workers are being told that they can't just drop what they are doing and get to schools and that schools will have special arrangements for their children. I tell her this is not a directive I have received and we do not have capacity of staff and space to look after symptomatic children for long periods. I raise this issue with Clare Kershaw during the morning's conference call. She will advise the Health Protection Board to correct this. Above all else, this expectation is plain wrong - health workers need to get home to isolate asap with their child, get them tested and wait for the results. Same rules for all.

Tuesday 8th September

The six and seven-year-olds have their first PE lessons. It is lovely to see the children filling the playgrounds with noise and laughter and getting lots of fresh air and exercise. Children have to wear their PE kits to school now. The downside of this practice is that outdoor PE lessons will be brought indoors if it starts to rain because we won't want the children to be sat in wet clothes for the rest of the day. A pity. There is something exhilarating about running about in the pouring rain!

Wednesday 9th September

Until we get the School running smoothly and everybody is used to the new arrangements and restrictions the wide range of Before and After School Clubs are on hold. The exception is the Sunrise and Sunset Clubs. These are a service for working parents. In the past demand has exceeded supply. Not this year. A sign of more parents working from home - or perhaps worse, having lost their jobs.

The Good Work Sharing Assembly worked remotely with children addressing the School from the classrooms and presenting slide shows on Zoom for all to see. The children have been thinking about the past six months, thinking about the positives of lockdown, what they missed most about School and what their hopes are for the coming year. That was fascinating. Their hopes range from the exotic, cuddle a koala bear, to the prosaic, going to the opticians.

Conference Call with County Hall - budgets. There is no good news. I make the point that schools face great challenges. After years of under-funding budgets are already tight. There are three new pressures facing schools. 1. Additional ongoing costs of keeping schools Covid-secure. 2. Schools income generating and fund raising streams have all but dried up. 3. The Government has said that schools will have to find the money to honour staff pay rises from our existing budgets. Yet again, the sums don't add up. I was pleased to be told that ECC meet with Essex MPs regularly and they are briefed in full of this worrying message.

The PM addresses the Nation this afternoon to introduce The Rule of Six - the maximum amount of adults who can meet together.

Thursday 10th September

I send an email to all parents, entitled,

Autumn Term Week 1 – the Covid Story So Far:

Dear Parent and Carers,

As the Government announced new measures yesterday, I thought it might be a good time to give you an update on life in (and out) of school.

I am pleased to report that parents are being very cautious. A few children are being kept off school as they are symptomatic. This is absolutely the right thing to do. The children are getting tested and the household is isolating until the results come back, hopefully negative.

Please let us know as soon as you get these results - negative and positive so that we can act quickly. Email and ansaphone are 24 hour services.

We will not inform parents of suspected cases, and we will never disclose names.

There will also be situations where children - and staff - cannot attend school because a member of their household is isolating. This will happen. I must repeat advice I have shared with you already – there may be times when it will not be possible to open every class because of staff shortages.

All adults - parents, staff, Governors must play their part by following all the new rules around social distancing - in the playground and in general life.

Please follow the rule of 6 - why wait until Monday. The virus won't!

This evening I am told that parents have not been able to get tests for their symptomatic children. One family has to drive to Norwich tomorrow. This won't do. We have been told that the only way we can contain this virus, without a total lockdown, is through a swift test and trace system. If people have to wait for tests, people who might be positive, they may have infected others who will still be going about their daily business. We will never get on top of it. Then, of course, there is the other issue of people travelling miles, if they can, when they are unwell. This is not a 'world-beating' system.

Our five-year-olds meet their new teachers for the first time. They will move up to their new classes on the 22nd. Ordinarily we would be inviting parents into school to meet the teachers too. This year the teachers will be making video presentations to introduce themselves.

Friday 11th September

The week finishes on a high with the rest of the children having their Meet The Teacher sessions. Chatting in the playground with parents doing the pick-up. We stand in the glorious sunshine discussing what Christmas in School will look like this year. Bazaar? Carol Concerts? Plays? Parties?

Get home. Watch the news. It is announced the R rate is above 1. Maybe the week doesn't finish on a high.

Year 1's meeting Mrs. Watson

Monday 14th September

The week gets off to a great start with an uplifting assembly thanks to a video made by one of our class of six-year-olds. I then meet with my Office Manager. We go through the names of all the pupils and staff who are symptomatic and awaiting tests, and those that are isolating because of symptomatic householders. No positives. We log the first date of absence. We will be holding these meetings daily for the foreseeable future.

Tuesday 15th September

Attendance rates are averaging about 92% so far. Slightly higher than the national average this Term.

After School the teachers enjoy a detailed presentation from our two Year 6 teachers who have been researching the resourcing and practical challenges of providing remote learning for our pupils who are well but unable to attend School. Teachers are left with mixed feelings. Whilst it was really helpful, it flagged up the difficult workload issues that 'blended learning' (as it is being called), will present.

Wednesday 16th September

30°C. In mid-September. Amazing.

Spend the afternoon in a conference call with our European special educational need project partners. The Italians cannot understand why everybody in schools in the UK does not have to wear masks, as they do. The Finns approach is different – they do not have to. The original purpose of the call was to finalise the programme and arrangements for the project finale to be held in the University of Parma next week. The conference will now be held remotely. Deadlines were not allowed to be extended. We will have to hold a four-hour technical rehearsal one evening next week.

Parents, desperate to work, are having to isolate with their children until they get a test and await the result. The mounting problems with the testing system are a potential source of tension between home and school. I email this letter to parents:

I understand your frustration. The one thing that everybody agrees on today is that the testing system is not working. This is creating great tension between families and school. You are not the only family questioning what is happening at the moment.

GP's, NHS 119, test and trace call centres and Public Health England are receiving thousands of calls and it would appear that they are giving contradictory advice to what the Government has instructed schools to do. Even more frustrating, sometimes these same organisations are giving different advice to different people even though their circumstances are the same.

As you will know from my communications with parents and the school risk assessment on the website, if a child shows one of the three symptoms then we must send the child home and instruct the parent to get a COVID19 test done for the child.

Let us hope that the test and trace system does improve otherwise this situation will occur continuously in every school across the country.

The Health and Safety Executive has been tasked with asking schools if they are covid-secure. They have outsourced this work and the office inform me that somebody will ring tomorrow at 10.30 for a ten minute phone interview.

Thursday 17th September
Today is the final day the children will spend with their teachers from last year. There is a strange End of Term buzz in the playground with children bringing in gifts for their teachers – which have to be stored in a Covid-secure way! By now all the parents should have seen the new teachers' videos of introduction as it is not possible to hold parent meetings in school.

I sit around waiting for the Health and Safety phone call. Didn't happen. I start another conference call with the Local Authority. Main topic of conversation was yesterday's announcement that the DfE will take hold of the communication system for schools reporting positive cases. Apparently local Health Boards can't cope with demand and respond quickly enough. The solution is not to improve capacity of these boards, of which there must be a few dozen, but to get all the schools across the country to ring one number in the DfE instead. As I understand it, if you get through, the call is triaged and then passed on to the local Health Board who then contact the school. How does that speed things up?

The Local Authority inform schools that we can still ring them direct. That is what I will do first, if necessary.

Friday 18th September
Only our Nursery and Reception are open today. The rest of the School are preparing for the new classes starting next week. Cleaning, timetabling of support staff, information sharing and briefing about pastoral care, individual and group support programmes are all finalised. Limitations on staff movements adds many layers of difficulty but there is a collective determination to get things right.

Unbelievable. I have my Health and Safety phone interview. I ask my questions first. Where is the proof that this person is legitimate? No paperwork was received in advance. Advised him to tell his line manager they should address this oversight. Is he expected to have looked at my School website to check all our Covid documents first? No. So he knows nothing about my School. I could tell him anything. He then proceeds to ask me a few multiple-choice questions. What a waste of time and taxpayers' money. I would like to know the cost of that contract.

Spend the end of the day in a Microsoft Teams call with the Local Authority's School Effectiveness Partner (SEP). A different conversation to the one I had with the Health and Safety Executive (HSE) person in the morning. In stark contrast, this detailed conversation with somebody who knows the School well covered all aspects of school operations and explored practical ways in which the School could be helped if required. Very constructive dialogue at no additional cost to the taxpayer. Afterwards I ask the NAHT to make a Freedom of Information request to find out what the HSE outsourcing contract has cost.

5.30pm. Just about to go home. The School cleaning team - a family business - are informed they have a symptomatic son. They reluctantly go home to self-isolate until the test is taken and comes back negative (hopefully). I now need practical help. Wonder if the SEP fancies cleaning some toilets and classrooms next week?

Monday 21st September

Only Nursery, Reception and Year 6 in School today. The Reception children stay for their first school lunch. Year 6 move into their new classrooms in their new uniforms for the first time. They look very smart and very proud. Parents are taking photos in the playground. The rest of the staff (Year 1 - Year 5) are preparing for their new classes' first day tomorrow.

No news on the cleaners' test result. His family remains isolated. Email goes out to staff to ask for volunteers to stay behind to do the cleaning duties for today in the first instance.

Mike Gogarty joined the Conference Call this morning with the Local Authority. He is candid: testing is an issue but Essex are working hard to increase capacity and turnaround and all education setting staff and their families are being prioritised. He wants schools to continue to ring the Essex number because he wants to 'test this team' to make sure they can meet the demand which will rise through the Autumn and Winter. (Apparently there have been some issues with the DfE helpline - who would have thought?)

I asked him about coughs because last Friday, Dr Hilary, on ITV's Good Morning Britain, told the nation to send their kids to school with coughs because it is normal and other medical organisations are advising that parents etc. should distinguish between a dry and phlegmy cough. I do not want to be stood on the School gate making these medical judgement calls. Mike said the PHE position remains that children should not come to School with coughs but get a test and stay home until the result comes back. And if a child has a cold (runny nose) with a high temperature then the temperature means a test has to be taken. He says the same applies to a child who is asthmatic: if the child with asthma develops a cough, they must have a test. That message could not be clearer.

Volunteers come forward. The school will be clean!

Tuesday 22nd September

Music lessons resume today. The music studio ceiling restoration has been completed. It is lovely to hear the sounds travelling across the infant courtyard. The lessons are slightly shorter to allow the Music Teacher to clean all the instruments in between use.

The Governors' Personnel Committee meet to review the pay policy which needs to be implemented from September 1st. We can only agree in principle because the Government is still to get the policy signed off in Parliament.

The Prime Minister addresses the nation. He announces a few measures which could be in place for six months. No new directives for schools.

Wednesday 23rd September

Parents inform me at the School gate that they can't complete the online registration of their children for the flu vaccine. Have we given parents the wrong information they ask? Our Office Manager finds out that the problem is demand. The system has been overwhelmed. They ask us to advise parents to be patient and persevere. She sends an email to all parents to do just that. Later a grandparent asks if this is a Covid vaccine. If only. The take-up for the flu vaccine since it was introduced a few years ago has been very high. Let's hope that it remains so. One concern. A side effect is a high temperature. How will parents distinguish between a high temperature as a reaction to the vaccine and Covid symptoms? Will check with Public Health.

The Local Authority send an email to all schools to strengthen their message that they want us to report positive cases to them and not the DfE because the advice coming from the DfE has not been good.

Thursday 23rd September

Ofsted are not resuming their full inspections until January. In the meantime, they have started doing 'informal' visits to schools. I tell the Local Authority that I am concerned that schools will come under pressure to prepare for these at a time when they should be totally focusing on keeping the school running at full capacity. I told the Local Authority that these 'coffee mornings' are a diversion and a distraction and I hoped they were not going to act in a way to heighten anxiety, like other authorities reportedly have been making schools be Ofsted prepared and even offering mock inspections. I was reassured by the response.

Amanda Spielman, Head of Ofsted, made a speech today issuing a warning that expectations on schools and families need to be realistic when it comes to schools' remote learning offer. Teachers are working flat out in school. More and more parents will be working from home. We all need to be realistic about what is possible. This was welcome. I hope the DfE and her own inspectors were listening. I spend the afternoon in conference with our Special Educational Needs Co-ordinator and the Educational Psychologist and Inclusion Partner assigned to the School by the Local Authority. Sadly, we have to share them with 30+ other schools. We flag up our concerns about how it is harder to use our staff efficiently because we can't put children from different classes into the same teaching groups. We focus our attention on new arrivals without support plans and children who will be moving to secondary school in 2021 and 2022. We need money to pay for the support essential for the new pupils to thrive and we need to catch up with the annual review backlogs and secondary application and transition work for the older pupils.

Friday 24th September
For years school staff and pupils across the UK have benefited from our participation in European Union funded education projects. Today, I 'attended' the final conference of the three year project. I have gained so much from those experiences and I have been proud to share with my school community and beyond. I will never forget visiting Oodi, the new Helsinki library - a library which is so much more than a library. 'Oodi is our shared living room. We are all responsible for keeping it comfortable.' It is an extraordinary place with all generations making full use of all Oodi's resources and amenities. Helsinki residents were involved in the design, demonstrating a commitment to social inclusion and civic pride that is truly remarkable. We visited that library at a time when libraries in England were being closed because apparently the sixth richest country in the World could not afford to keep them open. What a contrast in social, cultural and educational ambition.

The project produced valuable research into language acquisition difficulties and how to address them. Forging links with educationalists in other countries can only be a good thing. Tragically, schools across the UK will no longer be able to take part in projects such as these because we are no longer in the EU.

I am hearing that other local schools have a number of staff isolating and are struggling to keep all classes open. So far we have been lucky. Fingers crossed.

Oodi, the new Helsinki Library

Monday 28th September 2020

Our 60 Reception children stay for their first full day. The first of over a thousand over the next seven years. The Reception Team have made up goodie bags for parents, complete with a little poem. They can take these home and have a relaxing cup of tea and a biscuit whilst their children play and learn. It is a lovely, thoughtful idea.

Tuesday 29th September

The Office Manager checks with Health about the flu vaccine and how parents distinguish between vaccine side-effects and Covid symptoms.

Now is the time that parents are making decisions about secondary school applications. Guided tours and roadshows are out of the question. The roadshows are virtual, tours are virtual and parents are arranging their own remote Q&A sessions.

Teaching teams meet after School to finalise their plans for remote learning. This is for children who are not ill but unable to attend School for Covid-related reasons. I send out an email to parents in preparation. Expectations need to be realistic for parents and for teachers.

The *remote learning offer* cannot be as interactive as lockdown remote learning - it is impossible for teachers to teach their classes every day and provide an equivalent full day's home learning and respond to all the children's and parents' messages (as they did throughout lockdown). After all, it might be the teacher who is ill. And teachers will not be setting work on the first day of absence - this is a day when families will be trying to get tests or organising their own work and the household to prepare for what could potentially be a 14 day isolation period.

Wednesday 30th September

Now that our youngest cohort are attending full-time, they walk past me at the gate every morning. I am saying 'hello' to lots of parents and children that I do not recognise as we did not have all the normal meetings and transition events.

Write those parents a letter:

I have been hearing great things about your children... and you too! The Reception Team tell me that the children are gaining in confidence by the day as their indoor and outdoor learning environments become more familiar to them. They are separating from you without any wobbles. The Team are also really pleased with how you are getting into the swing of using Tapestry - which is such a great way to share learning - even more so as we will not be able to let you into school this term to join in lessons. Personally, I am finding it strange not having met you all as I would normally have done. At the moment I only get to see you in passing at the back gate. Apologies for not recognising those of you who are new to the school. I am sure that over the next seven years we will get to know each other very well.

This cohort will see me through to my retirement!

The DfE has done it again. This afternoon, after being quiet for months on the subject of remote learning, they publish their Temporary Continuity Direction. I naively believed this was going to be practical advice and guidance on how schools can manage remote learning. Instead the document announces its purpose is to provide *'legal certainty'*. It talks of a school's 'legal duty'. It comes into force from October 22nd. The tone is all wrong. We do not need to be told what our duty is.

Thursday 1st October
Raise the Temporary Continuity Direction with the Local Authority. They are going to be sending out separate advice and guidance to primary and secondary schools around remote learning.

Also ask about classroom temperatures. Now that the weather has turned properly Autumnal, ventilated classrooms can be quite fresh - although 30 children equal 30 little radiators producing their own source of heat. We know what the law says about minimum workplace temperatures, what does Public Health say about room temperatures in relation to Covid? And schools will be cranking up their boilers to pump out enough heat to maintain those temperatures through the day. This will be a massive additional cost to the School and not particularly environmentally friendly. I am told I will have to wait until Monday for answers to these questions.

Friday 2nd October
A team of nurses arrive to give children and staff their flu vaccines. About 2/3rds of the children will be having it - a little lower than previous years. Fifty-four staff have signed up. We always give staff a free vaccine. This is a sound investment. In previous years, staff who have not had the vaccine have had more time off work through the Winter. And this year we are told that if you have the flu vaccine, although it obviously won't protect you from getting Covid, it is likely to reduce the severity of the illness if you do catch it. Given that fact and given that we are told school staff are key workers it is disappointing to be told by other Heads that there are not enough vaccines for all their staff, and worse, some schools have been told there are no vaccines for their staff at all. That is not clear thinking. Hopefully it will be addressed.

Send an email to parents:
If your child has had the flu vaccine before you will know that a possible side effect of the vaccine is a high temperature...We have checked with the experts and their advice is as follows...If somebody (and this could be staff as well as pupils) does develop side effects of a high temp this will last between 24 and 48 hours...So, what should you do on Monday morning if your child still has a high temperature? The advice is that if a child still has a high temperature on Monday, they should stay off school and get a test...Fingers crossed that the children do not have these side effects but if they do that they do not last until Monday.

Fingers crossed for the staff too!

Covid tests, masks and school meals

North Primary School headteacher Alan Garnett shares his latest diary

■ Meals - Marcus Rashford led the school meals campaign

a request to all parents and the chair of the North School Association will write a letter to all the children. What was agreed was an ambition to do something to help families in need this Christmas.

Tuesday October 20
~~Yesterday and today was~~

It is a horrible feeling having to tell staff and parents that a period of 14 days isolation begins

Monday October 19
Walk to the gate this morning armed with a box of disposable masks in case any

Monday 5th October

A good start to the week. My worries about staff absence due to the potential side effects of the flu vaccine were unfounded. All aboard. No adverse effects amongst the children either. Major relief.

Children's University, (CU), bronze, silver and gold certificates were presented to children in this morning's Zoom Assembly. They should have graduated at the University of Essex, in the Ivor Crewe Theatre last Spring. Presenting the certificates today gave me the opportunity to explain to the children how the CU will work this year. The passport getting stamped for the time spent attending out of school hours activities won't work this year so the CU has gone online. It is creating a whole range of activities for which the children can earn credits. I encourage all children to join. The School pays the CU membership fee thanks to our Free For All charity.

I also launch the harvest appeal. The first Half-Term always ends with the School's Harvest Festival. Traditionally children walk into the Assembly Hall and donate a gift and Year 6 School Councillors create a magnificent display for all to see. A guest of honour makes a speech of thanks, explaining why there is a need for the charity and what difference the children's gifts will make. Special thoughts are shared and songs are sung. This year will have to be a little different but we will do our best in our class bubbles, joined as one via Zoom. The charity we will support is the Colchester Foodbank. Sadly, the Foodbank is needed more than ever. It even has a shop opposite our School which not only provides food parcels, it also has a supply of baby clothes and school uniform.

Tuesday 6th October

Teachers finalise their organisation of the Remote Learning Offer which I summarise into one document covering all age groups and email to parents. There are currently about a dozen children off school at the moment who are fit enough for school but isolating whilst a family member is tested. There does not seem to be any recognition in the DfE that managing remote learning whilst teaching a class full-time is significantly adding to workload.

Wayne Setford manages our garden. But he does so much more than that in Colchester. He is a local hero, creating so many opportunities for people in our community. The kids love him. The younger ones used to visit his community garden in High Woods Country Park. He will be coming back in soon but he will only be able to work with children from one class at a time. He sent me a clip of a film that has been made about a project he led through the Summer. The project was called *Together We Grow*. The film itself will be premièred at Firstsite in November. The clip is magical. Can't wait to see the whole film.

Wednesday 7th October

Zoom meeting with Governors this morning to check over the finances. Loss of income from lettings, clubs and fund-raising events; slight fall in pupil numbers; extra money required to be spent on (thoroughly deserved) staff pay rises, and ongoing costs of making the School *Covid-secure*. It will be the same for all schools. According to the Institute for Fiscal Studies the extra money the Government has promised over the next three years will not be enough to address the real-terms decline in school budgets. Last month the IFS published a report which said that school spending per pupil in 2022–23 would be no higher in real terms than in 2009–10. Very depressing.

Thursday 8th October

The infection rate appears to be growing exponentially around the country. Essex still has one of the lowest although it is also rising. The Government is talking about traffic lights and *'Tiers of Intervention'*. What will this mean in Colchester? As Half-Term approaches there is also talk of *'circuit breakers'*. Will schools be shut for two weeks and not one? There is much uncertainty.

Friday 9th October

Spent the day attending virtual meetings and conferences. The highlight was having the privilege to listen to Dame Alison Peacock. She spoke more sense in a few minutes than most manage over the course of their careers. She is the Chief Executive of the Chartered College of Teaching, has had a long and distinguished career in education and is a voice of influence in the corridors of power. She feels very strongly that schools should be focussing all their attention on meeting the challenge of remaining open for all pupils. She talked of the 'irrelevance of Ofsted' which will be a massive and unnecessary distraction at this current time if full inspections resume in January. Let's hope her message is being heard loud and clear.

Monday 12th October

The daily 'headcount' with the Office Manager is 16. That is the number of children out of 429 who are not able to attend school for Covid related reasons. Three staff are also off, waiting test results for themselves or a child. Two do not work on Mondays so hopefully the results will come back quickly and come back negative of course.

After School discuss with Senior Leadership Team whether face coverings need to be worn by parents. Ask the same question of the Governors in the evening curriculum meeting. Broad agreement. I will introduce it after Half-Term.

The Prime Minister announces that the country will be divided into either medium, high or very high-risk areas, with a sliding scale of measures for each tier. Based on our R rate, Essex is likely to be medium.

Tuesday 13th October

ECC has announced that it has asked the Government to be put in the high-risk tier with the aim of stopping the rise of the R rate. A brave call, not universally acclaimed but I commend their efforts to be proactive and learn the lessons of the first wave. I presume the Government will agree to the request. In line with this move, perhaps I should bring the face coverings decision forward a week.

Wednesday 14th October

The day begins with a lovely Good Work Assembly. A Year 6 class show off their self-portraits teaching the younger children the process as well as their finished works - I tell them these are the highest standard I have ever seen. The Year 1 class teach the school sign language for emotions. Lovely.

Join a crowdcast at 5pm on the subject of school funding. A wide range of speakers depress and inspire. The picture is bleak but the coalition of voices across the political, professional and stakeholder spectrum gives hope. Throughout the crowdcast I need the sign language for angry, sad and calm. No use for happy at the moment.

Thursday 15th October

Bad news. It is finally confirmed that delays with the design and procurement process mean that the essential works required to get the kitchen up and running again will not happen before the Christmas break. For a number of our families the children's midday meal is the only hot meal they get. Missing out on this during the warmer days of September and October has been a frustration. Missing out through November and December is not acceptable.

Furthermore, the kitchen continues to lose money because our numbers have taken a hit - paying parents don't want to pay for a pack-up. They can provide that from home - what they can't provide is a hot meal during the school day.

I inform staff and Governors the decision to introduce the wearing of face coverings for parents from Monday.

Friday 16th October
At 9.15 this email is sent to parents:

Dear Parents and Carers, Staff and Governors,

I think the first Half-Term has gone as well as we could have hoped. Parents, children and staff have adapted to all the new rules and procedures. Thank you all.

There has only been one positive case confirmed within our school community so far (a parent) which has meant that all classes have remained open. Planning can only take you so far – good fortune is always helpful. Long may that continue.

As you know, we constantly review our procedures and there are two changes that you need to know about. When winter arrives everybody - young and old - become more prone to illness which is not only likely to affect the R rate but may also worsen the impact of Covid on those who are unfortunate enough to catch it.

You will also be aware that Essex County Council wants to keep the virus under control and has asked the Government to designate the county as HIGH RISK. It has been confirmed that Essex will be Tier 2 (High Risk) from midnight tonight.

It is in this context that the following measures are being introduced.

1. All visitors coming inside the school buildings now have to wear face coverings – this applies to everybody - deliveries, contractors, specialists and parents.
2. From Monday 19th October it will become a school rule that all adults doing the school run must wear a face covering whilst in the school grounds.

We do still want you to: observe the rule of one adult per family on the site unless there are exceptional circumstances; observe the rule of 6, and social distance in the playground.

Thank you. I look forward to your co-operation.

Only one positive case so far! Spoke too soon. 11.25am get an email from a parent. Her child's test result has arrived - positive! Office Manager and I get ready to phone Public Health contact centre. 11.29 get through. A few details given. Told somebody will ring me back in 5-10minutes. After 20 minutes ring again. Apology received. Someone will ring soon. I know they will tell me to send the class and their staff home. I want to get this organised and the children collected asap - certainly before the end of the school day. Decide to inform the parents now. Run this past our SEP. He agrees. Emails and text messages sent. The class are informed. They are reassured that their classmate is OK. They stay in their classroom, eating their lunch and wait for their parents.

One hour and forty-five minutes after my initial call I receive the call I need from the Essex track and trace centre. I receive an apology for the delay. Lots of questions. When was the pupil last in School? Tuesday. Which staff worked with the class on Monday and Tuesday? That tots up to six: the class teacher, support assistants, midday assistant, IT technician and a supply teacher who covered Monday. It is confirmed that they will all have to isolate for 14 days, starting from the 13th. This means they will all be confined to their homes through next week and the start of the School Holiday. Remote Learning for the class.

Letter emailed to the parents of the class explaining what they must now do. Another email sent to the rest of the parent body keeping them informed.

I hold a special Zoom assembly at 2.40pm to let all the pupils know what is happening.

Open the School gates at 2.55, wearing my mask for the first time to advertise what will happen from Monday. Many parents have read their emails already. A sombre mood in the playground.

Monday 19th October 2020

Walk to the gate this morning armed with a box of disposable masks in case any parents have forgotten – or perhaps have objections to wearing one - that they now need to wear one to enter the site. I did not expect it to be a big issue. One parent had emailed to express her concerns but 100% compliance.

Late morning, we receive a phone call - a child in a Year 2 class has tested positive. She is OK. It is a horrible feeling having to tell staff and parents that a period of 14 days isolation begins – especially as it wipes out the holiday for them all. I get through to the DfE phone line first. They confirm that I do need to send the class home. They will email our local Health Board who will be in touch. At what point will I be instructed to close the School? Guidance had suggested that two cases could be viewed as an outbreak. Essex Contact Track and Trace Team ring in the afternoon. No further action – the virus is not out of control within the School. But there is definitely a growing number of cases in the local community.

The NSA (the School's parent teacher group) hold an evening Zoom meeting. Lots of head scratching: how can we bring the community together and generate income under the current restrictions? There are no easy answers. The decision is made to involve everybody in this group think. I will send out a request to all parents and the Chair of the NSA will write a letter to all the children. What was agreed was an ambition to do something to help families in need this Christmas.

Tuesday 20th October

Yesterday and today was spent meeting - face-to-face or remotely - with senior leaders (two of whom are now isolating) for their Performance Management. They talk as one, praising the brilliant job teachers in their teams are doing to tailor the curriculum to meet the identified needs of the classes in resourceful and innovative ways. And it is not just the teachers. All the staff at North have been incredible. Giving of their own time, working through lunch breaks and break times doing additional or different – and not always pleasant - duties. And now in some cases, accepting with grace their need to isolate for 14 days which includes a holiday period. They have been remarkable.

Got the chance to read the proofs of the CXXV book of the School's history. It is fantastic. Laura Davison (Project Co-ordinator) and Claire Driver (Project Historian) have done an unbelievable job. A wonderful tonic. Can't wait to write the preface and hold the actual book.

No class sent home today!

Wednesday 21st October
In assembly I tell the children about the book.

Colchester Foodbank get in touch. They will be providing food parcels for all families on our Free School Meals register - if they want them. The expansion of the Colchester Foodbank over the years is impressive and sad. I have been doing some research in preparation for the Harvest Festival that is supporting the Foodbank. Their capacity has grown exponentially over the past few years in direct response to the spiralling levels of need.

No class sent home today!

MPs vote this evening not to continue to provide food vouchers for families in need in England during school holidays. Marcus Rashford's campaign in the Spring shamed the Government into a U-turn. Will it happen again? I hope so.

I receive a phone call from a teacher at 9pm. He has received an email from a pupil with confirmation of a positive test result. She has not been in school all week. Contact Centres close at 8pm. I email parents of that class:

The School has just been informed that a child in the class has received a positive test result. We will be seeking the advice of Public Health first thing in the morning. We will let you know immediately of their decision. Until you receive that information your child should not leave the house in the morning.

I send out a similar email to staff who have been working with that class.

Thursday 22nd October
Get to School at 7.00am. Leave a message on the Essex contact team's ansaphone to ring me urgently - they open at 8.00am. Ring my SEP to see if he can do anything his end to help get my call prioritised. Still no call when I go to open the School gates at 8.20am. Stopped in my tracks, the phone rings. The decision: the child who tested positive had not been in School during the critical 48-hour period before the test was taken. Therefore, there is no reason for the children and staff in the class bubble to isolate for 14 days. Huge relief.

Email staff the good news and send an email to those parents...
... the class could be in school today. I hope you will understand why I made the decision last night. Imagine if I'd been told at 8.30 this morning that the class should be kept away. There would have been chaos at the school gates!

In my Thursday conference call with the LA and the Unions I pass on my experiences of the Essex Contact Track and Trace Centre. Advice is good but the response time is too long and it would be even more helpful if their phones were open for longer.

Apparently there are moves to increase capacity and extend opening hours. Good to hear.

School Photographer on site. Covid measures in place. Individual photos are taken. Not possible to take family photos this year. Mixing bubbles not allowed – although obviously at home they do mix! Photographer will come back to take photos of absent classes once they have returned.

Walking through the playground at lunchtime, a Year 5 boy passes and asks me how I am. Tell him that I am great, thank you very much. He replies, '*Is that because you have been reading the book again?*' What a lovely thing to say. My day is made.

Full Governing Body Zoom meeting this evening. Chair of Governors will write a letter of thanks to the staff.

Friday 23rd October
I inform the parents that I have postponed the Harvest Festival until after Half-Term. I email them, thanking them for their generous donations of food and toiletries and informing them that:

These occasions are a time when all the children celebrate together - even if they are sat in their own classrooms. Sadly, as you know, two classes are not able to attend school this week so I decided to wait until they come back. The special assembly will now take place on Monday 2nd November. Fortunately the director of the Colchester Foodbank, Michael Beckett, will still be able to attend.

NSA letter is sent out for parents to share with their children:

As you know, one of the impacts of the Coronavirus on school life in 2020 has been the cancellation of NSA events such as the disco, bingo and spring fair. We now know with certainty that we also won't be able to hold the annual Christmas Bazaar, which has always been a great opportunity to get together and celebrate, as well as raising money for the Free for All programme. It's a great shame not to be able to hold the Christmas Bazaar, but we also know that the safety of students, families and the wider community must come first.

As mentioned in Newsline, we now want your help to think of some ideas of how we might be able to celebrate Christmas without needing to meet-up in person. Perhaps it's a virtual Christmas quiz or bingo, a virtual treasure hunt, or some sort of Christmas gift exchange at the school? We know you'll come up with some great ideas, and we would be really grateful if you could share them with us by email with the subject line 'FAO NSA.' Alternatively, you can talk to your teacher, who can pass ideas onto the NSA.

We would like to take this opportunity to wish you a restful and safe Half Term. You are all doing a tremendous job at managing in these difficult circumstances, and hopefully we will be able to hold our school events again in the not too distant future.

3.00pm. End of Half-Term. I send all the remaining classes home!

'Rule of two will prove a challenge'

Monday, November 2

ALL classes are back in school today as the autumn half-term two begins. Children and staff from two classes spent part or nearly all of the holiday isolating. No new cases were reported over the holiday. But the spectre of lockdown two hangs over us all following the PM's announcement on Saturday evening that England would return to lockdown from Thursday until December 2. This time schools will remain open in full but we will have to wait for the updated guidance to know how of any changes to we will have to implement. What we do know is that we are moving from the rule of six to the rule of two which will prove a real challenge on the school run.

The day starts with our Harvest Festival. It was a very different occasion this year. Guest of honour Michael

■ Zoom call - Michael Beckett, Colchester Foodbank CEO

■ **Column: North Primary School headteacher Alan Garnett reflects on the challenges posed by keeping his school open during the second national lockdown**

The inspectors were impressed with the measures in place. They said schools are doing a tremendous job

Monday 2nd November

All classes are back in School today as the Autumn Half-Term 2 begins. Children and staff from two classes spent part or nearly all of the holiday isolating. No new cases were reported over the holiday. But the spectre of lockdown 2 hangs over us all following the PM's announcement on Saturday evening that England would return to lockdown from Thursday until December 2nd. This time schools will remain open in full but we will have to wait for the updated guidance to know any operational changes will be required. What we do know is that we are moving from the rule of 6 to the rule of 2 which will prove a real challenge on the school run.

The day starts with our Harvest Festival. It was a very different occasion this year. Guest of Honour Michael Beckett, CEO of the Colchester Foodbank, 'Zoomed' in to speak to the children and say a great big thank you for the generosity of the School community.

It is not the first time the School has supported the Foodbank. Michael told us why they are needed more than ever. Last year they gave out 9,400 parcels. This year they have already given out 13,000. Colchester Foodbank opened in 2008. It now has 10 distribution points and is the second busiest in the East of England, thanks to the commitment of 250 volunteers. Of course, they can only do this with the continued support and generosity of the people of Colchester and local businesses. The children learnt that foodbanks not only give out food parcels they also run holiday clubs and provide advice and support for people to help them turn their lives around. The children learnt that foodbanks were set up by a charity called the Trussell Trust. Their aim is to end food poverty in this country, but in the meantime, they work with people of all faiths and none, inspired by the words of Jesus:

For I was hungry and you gave me something to eat, I was thirsty and you gave me something to drink, I was a stranger and you invited me in, I needed clothes and you clothed me, I was sick and you looked after me, I was in prison and you came to visit me.

The Trust aims to make a difference—a value we promote every week through our Good Citizen Awards. The Foodbank really does make a difference.

Michael told the children they also have a brilliant campaign for November called the Reverse Advent Calendar. Every day in November add a food item. By the end of the month, you will have assembled a very nice parcel to give to the Foodbank in December. What a great idea.

Receive a phone call at lunchtime from an Inspector from the Health and Safety Executive (HSE). She and a colleague will pay the School a visit tomorrow afternoon to check our Covid-secure measures. She asks me to send over the School's risk assessment. On site she will need to speak with me, tour the School, speak to any Union reps.

Tuesday 3rd November
The HSE Inspectors arrived just after 1pm. The visit went well. They were impressed with the measures in place. They said that schools in general are doing a tremendous job. They were keen to find out what impact this is having on how the School runs. I told them that it is an inefficient use of staff, limiting the intervention work we do; there are ongoing additional costs which the Government refuses to cover, and that I am very concerned that we are two days away from lockdown and we still have not received the advice on what vulnerable children and adults should do. They said they would feed this back.

Wednesday 4th November
Emailed parents this morning.

Today is the last day before England moves into lockdown 2. Will this make any difference to how the School functions? Based on what we know at the present time the short answer is not really. But we are still awaiting detailed advice on what precautions the clinically extremely vulnerable should take. In the first lockdown the guidance meant that some children and staff could not attend school. That is why it is important that we get this information. Hopefully that advice will be published this week.

The one significant difference will be the 'rule of two'. Adults are only allowed to share fresh air with one other adult outside your household per day. This will present a challenge for you all on the school run and in the school grounds. Please do your best to observe this new rule. We do not want this lockdown to last any longer than four weeks.

3.30pm. At last. The guidance is published. The clinically vulnerable just need to be cautious and continue to follow all safety measures. The clinically extremely vulnerable (CEV) should isolate but their household members do not need to shield, which is different from Lockdown 1. The CEV can continue to go to work but must sign a disclaimer. That puts employees and employers in a very difficult position. However dedicated one is, personal health has to come first. This will put additional strain on schools trying to keep every class open. The only other change to guidance is the mandatory wearing of face coverings in communal areas in secondary schools. But as Essex has been in Tier 2 this precaution has already been in place.

Spend the evening attending a crowdcast organised by the National Association of Headteachers. Should Ofsted resume its full inspections from January as planned? A number of distinguished speakers made compelling cases against the resumption. Former Education Minister, Baroness Morris, and prominent educationalist Dame Alison Peacock, who has sat on many Government advisory boards, amongst them. I agree. Schools are working flat out trying to remain open and manage remote learning. On top of this, it just adds to the risk. A school in London last month had to close because an Ofsted Inspector tested positive. He hadn't been near the children but had been in lengthy conversations with a number of staff who then had to isolate. An unnecessary and unwelcome distraction.

Thursday 5th November
Lockdown 2 day 1. Glorious Autumnal sunshine. Email the parents.

The Government published its guidance for schools at 3.30pm yesterday outlining what should and should not happen in school during lockdown which started today. In primary schools we continue with all our established practices. The infection rate in primary age children is still currently very low. The advice for clinically vulnerable children and staff is to continue to come to school and adhere to all the control measures in place. The advice for CEV children and adults is to not attend school during lockdown. Remote learning will be set and staff will work from home. If you live with somebody who is CEV you do not need to isolate. You should continue to come to school. If you are not sure whether you fall into the CEV group please speak to your GP or clinician. If your child is in the CEV group please contact the school immediately.

Friday 6th November
Take stock of absentees. Probably the lowest number of children isolating this Term pending test results for them or family members. We have lost a few staff who will be isolating during lockdown because of their health conditions. Day spent finding temporary solutions to plug the gaps. We are stretched very thin.

Monday 9th November

Assembly is all about Florence Nightingale. Who would have thought that talking about her achievements would take on such a contemporary relevance? It was due to her influence that the first nurses' teaching hospital was established in London in 1860. Now we have emergency Covid hospitals built in her name. And '*the lady with the lamp*' was hugely influential in promoting the washing of hands as a principle of good hygiene and that hospital wards had to be well ventilated. Just like school classrooms today!

The morning is spent in contact with Anglian Water. Drain issues with neighbours has forced us to close the front pedestrian access until the source is identified and the clean-up operation completed.

Frustrating news received after School. A teacher has been told by NHS track and trace that she has to isolate for 14 days. Somebody she knows has tested positive. At some point this situation was likely to happen and with 70 staff we may have been lucky for it to have only happened to twice now. But it is a terrible nuisance. Supply teachers are in short supply at the moment.

The Prime Minister holds a Press Conference to announce that a vaccine is on its way. This is really good news.

Tuesday 10th November

The smell of hot food is wafting around the School again. And it is lovely. Staff and children comment as they pass by the kitchen. The work to replace the extractor fan hood has not started but we have hired a couple of electric ovens which has enabled the cooks to put on a limited hot food menu.

Wednesday 11th November

Zoom into an Essex Primary Head Association meeting. Hot topic – where is the money? Nationally schools on average have spent £9,000 to keep them Covid-secure. The Government is determined that we all stay open but is less enthusiastic about covering our costs, despite our already stretched budgets. There is a limited reimbursement scheme. It is limited. And it does not seem to be doing much reimbursing. Not acceptable.

At the 11th hour on the 11th day of the 11th month the children and staff at North Primary School and Nursery observed a minute's silence - wherever they were, whatever they were doing. 6A were on break and enjoying letting off steam in the woodland area. They stopped, paid their respects and then resumed their games.

In the Gazette yesterday there was a lovely article about a local family who live in a house which has one of our Poppy Plaques on its front wall. These plaques commemorate former pupils of North who lost their lives in the First World War. Pictured was the little girl, Willow, outside her house where there is not only our plaque, but also one that her mum has added. Willow may one day be a North pupil, and then she will be able to see the name of Ernest. C. Stowe on our roll of honour.

Received a bundle of postcards today from former pupils who are now attending St Helena Secondary School. The children have written to their old teachers and the current Year 6's to let them know how they are doing. It is a lovely idea and the postcards are great.

Thursday 12th November
Today the School celebrates its 126th birthday. Receive a birthday message from a dear friend of the school, Sir Bob Russell, who kindly passed on a Tweet from Colchester Civic Society: #OnThisDay - 12 November, 1894, North Street School - the first in #Colchester funded from local taxation - was opened. It cost £8,000. Not even enough money to keep us Covid-secure! I wonder how much it would cost to build this School today.

Conference Calls all day. Hot topics are Ofsted and exams. England is the only one of the four nations not to have announced any changes to the exam system for this academic year – apart from the shifting of dates. Apparently in the corridors of Whitehall there is an acceptance that there does need to be a rethink but that the decision will be made in No.10. By now we normally would have received test administration guidance and be booked on to moderator courses for the Spring Term. We are still waiting for the former and the latter have been cancelled. What should we read into this? Indecision and prevarication are so unhelpful.

Friday 13th November
The morning headcount of isolators is the lowest for some time but the infection rate is rising highest in the northern side of Colchester, part of which sits in our catchment area.

Another phone call is made about the drains – this time to a local Councillor. It is intolerable that we have had to shut our front pathway again.

Oh no. Phone call received from a parent of a child in Nursery. Positive test result. Inform the DfE and Essex Contact Track and Trace Team. Texts and emails sent to parents to collect their children. Staff sent home to isolate. Letters emailed to all parents, staff and Governors to explain the situation. Nursery will not open again until 26th November. Sad end to the week.

Monday 16th November 2020
A new week begins with all classes open but the Nursery is closed until the 26th. The front of the School is strangely quiet without the sounds of lots of little people playing outside.

Extraordinary times. The Conservative controlled County Council has written to the Conservative Government raising a number of concerns about this year's tests and exams and making three requests: urgency and clarity around the contingency arrangements for tests and exams for the 2021 cohort; that performance tables are suspended again for 2021; and that Ofsted do not reinstate full inspections in January 2021 due to the immense pressure on the education system at the moment. Totally agree. It is heartening to know that the Local Authority has a clear understanding of the challenges that teachers and students face. Let us hope that the Government is listening. I wonder what would happen if Headteachers took the perfectly reasonable decision to temporarily put the interests of their school community ahead of the judgement of Ofsted.

Dear Lead Inspector, I am proud of my school and I would ordinarily love to celebrate our achievements with you. However, I am going to have to politely and respectfully say 'no, thank you,' to your request to visit tomorrow. I would be happy to have a structured conversation over the phone or even Zoom once I have made sure that every class is open and all staff have reported for duty...

The NSA held its AGM this evening via Zoom. It was terrific. There were lots of new faces adding creativity and great energy to the group. There was a collective determination that although all the wonderful things that happen in a primary school through December can't happen, there are ways of making Christmas at North special for the children and their families. Inspiring.

Tuesday 17th November
Extraordinary times take 2. The DfE published guidance for schools today to prepare for the possible disruption to the food supply chain in January because of Brexit. It says:

You may need to consider whether changes are necessary. These might include: varying the timing and number of deliveries to allow for transport delays; being as flexible as possible on delivery times during the day; ordering longer shelf-life products during this period, such as frozen foods or foods that can be safely stored at room temperature.

Not sure where we are going to store all this extra food - school kitchens have limited storage capacity so we have two or three deliveries a week already. I presume the Government will not be giving this advice to the general public otherwise the supermarket shelves will be emptied within days!

Wednesday 18th November
The problem with the neighbour's drains has finally been identified. Colchester Borough's Environmental Health team pay a visit: they inform me the drain serving the flats in front of the school has collapsed. The work may take more than a day. Hopefully the work will get done before the end of the week so that the pedestrian access to the front of the School will not get polluted again. It is very fortunate that this entrance is not being used by Nursery families this week.

Thursday 19th November
Mike Gogarty joined today's conference call with the LA and Union representatives. He says it is still too soon to see the impact of Lockdown 2 on infection rates, but on average Essex is still well below the national average. He did share some depressing news about the track and trace system. He estimates that currently about 25% of positive cases are actually getting tested and only about 20% of people are isolating who should. In other words, the problem with the track and trace system is not just about supply and turnaround, it is also about public engagement and compliance. He also said that school staff would not be a high priority for the Covid vaccine as we do not work with vulnerable or high-risk groups. I understand that argument but on the other hand if schools are to remain fully open, they need all their staff able to turn up for work. Surely, if staff are vaccinated, they will not have to isolate if a member of their own household or a pupil in their class gets Covid. Similarly schools are still being told that all their staff cannot have the flu vaccine this winter. For schools to remain fully open we need all our staff fit and healthy.

I received a phone call this afternoon. One of the teachers is unable to come to work tomorrow. Her family have taken Covid tests. It will be an anxious wait now for the result.

Friday 20th November
The week finishes with some good news. The teacher and her family have tested negative. The Government announce that a vaccine may be ready during December. That is great news.

Monday 23rd November

A quiet start to the week. Not just because the Nursery remains closed. Just over half-way through Lockdown 2 and the number of children and staff in the School who are isolating is low. Let us hope that remains the case this week.

Tuesday 24th November

Tomorrow night we are holding a remote parents meeting. A big event. It is for parents of children who will be starting school in September 2021. They must submit online applications to the Local Authority by January 15th. They can name four schools in order of preference. It is a big decision for parents, some visit as many as eight schools. In normal times we invite parents into School for an evening meeting. They listen to a presentation from me and a presentation from the head of the Foundation Stage. We show a film of a day in the life of the Reception children and our oldest pupils present a talk. Afterwards these pupils are tour guides as parents are free to wander around the School and talk to staff and Governors. The title of the Year 6 talk is, 'What does seven years at North look like?' This was introduced a number of years ago. That Year 6 cohort created a slide show outlining all the things about North which they thought made it a special school. Of course, through their talk and the way they act as tour guides, the parents get to see the living proof of how North pupils turn out. It makes a wonderful impression. Each year the next Year 6 has tweaked and updated that talk. Our current Year 6 has done the same but recorded their voices as the event is being held via Zoom.

As the meeting will be Zoomed out live, we are keen to get the technology right. A technical run through is held after School. Documents are visible, films load, chat room works, sound is perfect. We are ready. What could possibly go wrong?

Wednesday 25th November

Two Governors' committees held Zoom meetings this morning. There is anger that the mess in our front pathway, caused by our neighbour's drain issues, took so long for them to rectify. I am instructed to find out whether the Council issued a warning to the neighbours and then write a letter of complaint to the management company. It has been extremely fortunate that the walkway has not been needed by the Nursery during this period but that is not the point.

7.00pm. Parents Meeting. We are all set. It is very strange talking to an audience that you cannot see and who you have not even met. When you teach, or address a meeting, you can see and sense the audience reaction, and adjust the presentation accordingly. Reading the comments in the chatroom is as close as we can get to that instant response.

Of course, you don't get any feedback if your microphone is on mute! Two slides in, a parent unmutes to say, '*Mr. Garnett, we can't hear you!*' Mortifying. It would seem that our technical run through did not provide the insurance we were hoping for and the meeting subsequently suffered from a number of embarrassing glitches. The parents were very understanding and, judging by their comments, got the information that they needed to help inform their decisions. *'Great presentation. We already have one child at North in Year 3 and he loves it. He still talks about his time in Mrs Arnold's / Mrs Ward's class - it was a great intro to school life for him. Thanks again.'* Another wrote. Having been informed that the Reception teachers have a combined 34 years of service to the School, *'It is very clear that there is a passion for the school and children from Mr Garnett and the teachers :) '*

All aspects of the presentation need to be recorded and popped onto the website.

Thursday 26th November

The Nursery re-opened today after the children and staff completed their 14 days of confinement. It was lovely to see and hear the children busy playing - *'there is nothing as serious as a child at play'.* That quote dates back to Ancient Greece. So true.

The Government announce that when lockdown ends next week Essex will be placed in Tier 2. Most of England will be in higher tiers than before lockdown. Was that the point of the sacrifices of the past month? Parliament must approve these plans first.

Albert enjoys his day at Nursery

Receive an email from a parent - will the children be allowed to give out Christmas Cards? A good question. Schools are limiting what children bring into school and what they take home. Most only give cards to children in their own class, who are in their own bubble of course, so that should be straightforward, but what about across bubbles? It is funny how seemingly minor issues like this can be banana skins. You can get all the big, tough and often unpopular decisions right and slip up over something which seems trivial.

Local Authority give an update on the lateral flow tests. Essex should have received delivery of 290,000 by now. Not one has arrived.

Attend an NAHT school leaders' conference in the afternoon. All indicators suggest the Government will make an announcement next week about Ofsted returning to full inspections in January and any changes to the exam and testing systems in England next summer. Let us hope those decisions show that Ministers and the PM have listened to the broad coalition of voices - professional associations, Unions, Governors associations, and local authorities, including Essex - which have expressed their well-informed opinions on these subjects.

Friday 27th November

The week finishes with the frustrating news that the kitchen work due to be completed during the Christmas Holidays will not be completed until mid-January.

Saturday 28th November

Email parents to explain the Christmas Card rules. We will not have the central school post-box. Children will be able to give out cards in their own classes. Cards for those beyond their classrooms will be stored and given out a few days later. I also share a poster which was kindly given to me by a parent with alternative suggestions to mass Christmas Card exchanges. Parents and children can also do what many staff do – instead of swapping cards we make a donation to East Anglian Children's Hospice, a charity we support every Christmas.

Receive an email from a member of staff who will not be able to come to School for a fortnight because their child, who attends a local school, has had their bubble sent home to isolate. This is going to leave a hole in our provision that will not be easy to cover.

Mrs. Fatama Miah, the Nursery re-opens

First snow on the sequoia tree, planted at the School Centenary in 1994

Zoom open days and festive cards

Daily Gazette, Friday 4 December 2020

Monday 30th November

In the field of observation, chance favours only the prepared mind.

The words of Louis Pasteur that I shared with the children in an assembly a couple of weeks ago. I introduced them to a new word - serendipity. Louis Pasteur's great discovery, which he named vaccine - after the work of Edward Jenner - was down to forgetfulness on the part of his assistant and then good observation and analysis on the part of Pasteur: serendipity. This word came up again in my assembly this morning because the company, AstraZeneca, announced the exciting news last week that their Covid vaccine has about a 90% success rate. Apparently, there was a mix-up in the trials that led to this high efficacy. Mene Pangalos, executive vice-president of biopharmaceuticals research and development at AstraZeneca, is reported as saying that, *'The reason we had the half dose is serendipity.'* Let us hope we are all able to benefit from this good fortune as quickly as possible.

After School the senior leadership team shared with me their Catch-Up plans for pupils who have fallen behind significantly with their learning over the past year. This year we are receiving £8,000 each Term from the Government Catch-Up Fund. A summary of these plans has to be posted on the School website. This will happen in the New Year.

Inform the Governors of these plans at their Curriculum Committee meeting this evening. They also want to know what is happening with statutory assessment and whether Ofsted will resume full-scale inspections in January. I tell them that I have been reliably informed that a decision is to be announced this week. All I know for sure is that ECC's letter to Gavin Williamson urging him to rethink Ofsted and league tables is yet to receive a reply.

Tuesday 1st December
Final day of Lockdown 2.

The Christmas season is officially starting in School. Teachers and children are beginning the serious business of decorating their rooms. Which class will be the inaugural winners of the Most Christmassy Classroom Competition? The trophy will be presented to the winners after judging on the 16th.

The NSA has bought licences for every class to have Disney+. This is a lovely treat and will make eating lunch in their classrooms a bit more joyful.

MPs vote to return to the tier system, albeit with tougher restrictions - Essex will be in Tier 2.

End the day with another evening meeting - Governors' Personnel Committee. I inform them that, once again, the dedication and effort of all the staff this Term has been amazing.

Wednesday 2nd December

When will School finish and the holiday begin for school leaders and office managers? And when will the Spring Term start? Questions I emailed to the Director of Education today ahead of our meeting tomorrow. The answer to the first question, seemingly, is Christmas Eve. Children or staff who are symptomatic on the final day of Term will need to get tested. Their results could take several days to come through, so Public Health are saying that schools could be notified as late as Christmas Eve. We would then have to inform families and staff of the requirement to isolate. That will be a popular message! Clearly, the track and trace system can't work without the support of schools. In other words, some school staff will be 'on call' that first week of their holiday.

And what will the start of the Spring Term look like? With a relaxation in the tier system over the Christmas period there is an expectation that cases will rise. Schools will be receiving emails and calls from New Year's Day onwards from staff and parents who are having to get tests and isolate. My question to the LA is: could the School Term start a day later so that schools can spend that Monday making sure that they have the capacity to open all their classes? Advanced notice will avoid last minute decisions that will cause disruption to working parents. It would also provide the reassurance parents need to know that schools are still safe.

All schools have been sent a certificate from ECC, signed by Cllr Ray Gooding and Clare Kershaw. It is the launch of their annual Teaching Awards competition but they also feel that all school staff are worthy of recognition now.

We are, however, very aware that every one of you and your community are our unsung heroes. You have demonstrated commitment, inspiration, resilience and agility and we are thankful for all that you are doing. Please find attached a certificate of our appreciation.

A nice touch.

Thursday 3rd December

Wake up to the news that Ofsted will not resume full inspections in the Spring Term. Nice to see common sense prevailing. It is also announced that there have been some changes to the testing system in Year 2, Year 4 and Year 6 but no news on the Foundation Stage. So tests and statutory assessment will go ahead but there will not be League Tables. The Junior Education Minister, Nick Gibb, has said repeatedly over the years that the reason for having Year 6 tests is to compare schools. Not this year, apparently. So, I am not sure what the purpose of Year 6 reading and maths tests will serve.

The smell of parkin, emanating from the kitchen, is wafting around the school. The cake's sweet, spicy warmth is the very essence of Christmas. And it tastes as good as it smells!

Long discussion with the LA in response to my questions about the end of this Term and the start of the next Term. The Director of Education is very sympathetic. Announcements will be made next week.

There is a PS from the DfE this evening - no change for assessment of the youngest in our School - the Early Years Foundation Stage Profile must be completed in the Summer Term.

Friday 4th December
Snow! Lots of it. It is laying but very soft and watery. The pavements in town and the School pathways and playground are not slippery just very, very wet. Send an email to parents advising that children should wear wellies and bring slippers.

The day finishes with a special visitor - remotely of course. Father Christmas 'Zoomed' in to deliver a message to all the children. He comes to our Christmas Bazaar every year. The children and staff loved seeing him although some of the older children tried to feign indifference to hide their excitement. Unsuccessfully. A magical way to end the week.

Father Christmas 'Zoomed' in to deliver a message to the children at North

Monday 7th December

Over the weekend preparation works finally started to get the kitchen running properly again. So, scaffolding is in place to enable access to the roof and loft spaces. Meanwhile underneath the School the cellar water pump has given up for good. It has sounded poorly for some time and the Site Manager had contacted a company a couple of weeks ago to fix it but they are still waiting on a part. We have a very high-water table and before the pump was fitted, earlier in my time as Head, if the nearby River Colne burst its banks water could flood the cellar, sometimes coming half way up the stairs. The pump kicks in to prevent that. Just as well now as we have a very high tech, brand new boiler system in place. Without the pump working over the weekend water is just covering the floor and is close to seeping over the step into the boiler room. The engineers need to come today otherwise we will be down there with buckets manually emptying the water into nearby drains.

Tuesday 8th December

Today will be known as V Day. People across the country, including Colchester, received the Covid-19 vaccine. One of the first was an elderly resident of Stratford-upon-Avon going by the name of William Shakespeare. Nice to start the day with a good news story.

The manager of the local OneStop convenience store presented me with a hamper for the School. She wanted to give it to the staff which was a lovely thought but we will add it to the prize for the Christmas Raffle.

Finally, the Government announce their recommendations for the end of Term, with just 10 days to go. Schools can turn the final day of Term into a non-pupil day if they want as long as they make up the day later in the year. Not having the children in School on the Friday would mean some staff would not be on call for the test and trace system on Christmas Eve. Just until the 23rd.

This is a worst-of-all-worlds decision. Too short notice for working parents. Too short notice to organise a proper staff training day. Of course, it is not only the DfE that have messed up. DHSC too. We only have this problem because the track and trace system is still so inefficient. If it was 'world beating' we would not be waiting until Christmas Eve to get results from staff or children who were symptomatic at the end of Term. Department for Education, Department of Health: a plague o' both your houses.

Wednesday 9th December

The day is spent organising the end of Term and the start of next Term. My decision is consistent with the Local Authority's guidance, published in the afternoon, and I get the approval of the Chair of Governors. Brief the teachers after School and send an email to parents in the evening.

Dear Parents and Carers,

You may have read reports about possible changes at the end of Term. There will be no change to the end of Term at North. We will finish on Friday 18th December.

The DfE finally made an announcement yesterday - far too short notice - they have been pressed to make a decision since October! The problem is the Track and Trace system. Firstly, it can't operate without schools' support. And, the system still takes too long.

This is what must happen during the holiday.

Parents and staff must please email the school if a child or school employee is taking a test. They must then email the school with evidence of the test result.

If the member of staff or pupil was symptomatic on the 17th or 18th of December and tests positive then I will have to inform parents and staff of the need to isolate for 14 days.

If symptoms develop during the holiday, then the procedure is the same because that will impact on the start of Term.

Start of Spring Term

The R rate is rising and that is before we enter the 5-day Christmas period when the rules are relaxed and we know that there will be a subsequent spike in Covid cases. This is likely to mean that staff, children and their parents may be waiting for test results, had positive results themselves or be in isolation because of a household member testing positive. This could lead to significant disruption at the start of Term. Therefore to remove all uncertainty, Monday January 4th will be a remote learning day. Teachers will set work for the children via Tapestry or SeeSaw. By making this decision now, it is hoped that working parents will have time to adjust.

Children will return to school on Tuesday 5th January 2021.

For those of you travelling abroad during the holiday period, the Government has said it will announce updated quarantine regulations on December 15th.

It is so important that we all follow all these rules. We do not want Essex to move into Tier 3 in January, or worse.

Thursday 10th December
Tomorrow in schools across the county, children and staff will be taking part in the Santa Dash. Our two oldest year groups do theirs today. They arrive in their PE Kits and Santa hats.

At the usual meeting with the LA at 11.00, it is clear that things are not going well in Basildon - the borough now has the sixth highest infection rate in the country. Schools and the LA are faced with some very tough decisions. Mobile testing units have been set up and lateral flow tests have finally arrived in Essex. On the 16th the Government will announce any changes to the tier system. There is a real concern that if Essex is seen as one area, then we could all move into Tier 3.

Our PE Teacher has calculated that collectively our Years' 5 and 6 ran 248 miles, which would get you all the way to Paris. How far will the rest of the School get us tomorrow?

Year 3 Santa Dash

Friday 11th December

The children have been made origami hearts for a special display. They could add messages if they wished. These four messages capture the mood: *I want to see Father Christmas; We want to help the foodbank; I hope that the vaccine for Covid-19 will be ready for everyone to use; I hope that next year is great.* There is also a cheeky one - '*Dear Family, have a brilliant 2021 and make more money.*'

With all the rain this morning Santa's Dash turned into Santa's Splash. The younger children were not deterred and collectively ran over 400 miles. Over the two days the children and staff ran 683 miles in total. As the sleigh flies that would get Santa's to Lillestrom in Norway - not quite all the way home.

At the end of the day the children filed out with their end of Term reports, as face to face consultations have not been possible. We normally say that there should be no surprises in the reports - simply confirmation of what has been said to parents already. Obviously that will not be the case this time. Let's hope there are not too many shocks!

Reception Santa Dash

Lola in the Christmas grotto

Entrance to the Christmas grotto

The Ingram family

Monday 14th December

Wow! Never Cease to Amaze. You are stood there like a proud Dad. Just some of the words from parents as they walked into School this morning. The NSA was thrilled with the children's reaction and the parents' lovely comments about the transformation to the Victoria Chase entrance which had been turned into a snow-themed grotto. The NSA was also delighted with the response to their origami heart challenge. Attaching the hearts to the snow camouflage was a painstaking job, made bearable by the lovely messages written on the hearts.

Grotto message

Huge credit must go to Wayne Setford, our gardener and inspiration behind Together We Grow. The grotto design was Wayne's vision. Quite brilliant. It took all of Sunday and an early start this morning to create the grotto. It was worth the effort.

It was announced today that the southern half of Essex would move into Tier 3. Colchester will remain Tier 2.

Tuesday 15th December

Yesterday we had local folk musicians Emma and Tom Hardy playing carols as the children emerged from the grotto as they entered the School grounds. Today they were greeted with a snow machine. Such excitement. It really was magical.

It was announced today that mass testing would be rolled out in the Borough of Basildon. But, despite massive spikes in infection rates in secondary schools, the Government is determined to stop schools moving to remote learning - issuing letters threatening legal action.

Wednesday 16th December

Local classical musicians, Sarah Mills and Nigel Hildreth, played the children into school today. Beautiful.

Through December children have been bringing in donations for The Colchester Foodbank. It has been well supported. This morning the Foodbank volunteers arrived with an empty van and left with a full one.

All schools received a Christmas present today. A 27-page booklet on how we will have to administer lateral flow tests to pupils and staff in the New Year. This arrived with absolutely no warning. No warning to schools. No warning to Local Authorities. No warning to Public Health Essex.

Thursday 17th December

Christmas Lunch Day. Children came to School wearing their Christmas jumpers and hats. Families were greeted by three members of the Colchester Accordion Showband playing Christmas songs whilst four Year 6's rattled buckets to encourage donations for the East Anglian Children's Hospice.

Unfortunately I could not enjoy the music because I was busy making sure a Year 3 class did not come into School. At 8.10 we received confirmation of a positive case in the class. At 8.12 parents were notified by email. I stood at the gates to make sure all the affected families had got the message. Well, ParentMail passed the test – only three families had missed the message. The children and staff connected to the class will be isolating at the start of the holiday. What miserable news.

More information is forthcoming from the Government. It is confirmed that they expect secondary schools and colleges to run the lateral flow testing programme in January. So that they can prepare to manage this health service, remote learning for most of their students must be offered at the beginning of Term. At some point in the future primary schools will also be administering the tests.

Well, this has been some week for the Department for Education. Over the past nine months we have got used to incompetence with the occasional dose of gaslighting. We have been taken for granted to keep the Test & Trace system operational during our holidays. Now Gavin Williamson has instructed the School Teachers Review Body not to award 'pay uplifts' to the majority of teachers. He has also intimidated LAs, trusts and individual schools by threatening to sue them. And not just those areas which made national headlines - Greenwich, Islington and Waltham Forest - but in Basildon too. To cap it all he now expects schools to provide a health service, to administer the Lateral Flow Tests. It is also announced that there is a 30-minute training webinar scheduled for tomorrow.

I love my job and I will do anything and everything that I can for the good of the children and my staff. And I think I have over the past nine months. But in my twenty years of Headship, I have never been so angry about a Government decision. (And over the course of this century there have been some pretty shocking initiatives foisted on schools by Governments of all colours in their efforts to micro-manage education.) There is not one element of this initiative that the Government has got right. As the plans exist, with the timeframe proposed, the scheme is inoperable. What makes this sorry state of affairs even more shocking is that the idea of mass testing as a preventative measure is a good thing.

Friday 18th December

The final day of the School Term and calendar year. Apart from the class isolating, the attendance has remained good this week. In general terms the health of children and staff has been better than in other Autumn Terms. Mike Gogarty, Head of Public Health Essex, did predict in the Summer that this would be the case as the Covid hygiene rules would bring wider benefits by reducing the spread of colds and flu. How right he was.

The Governors' Awards were presented in the final Zoom assembly of the Term. Two children from each class are commended for their effort, achievement and progress. After assembly I would normally take a group photo of the 28 children to put in the newsletter but bubble rules mean I have to take 14 photos.

Also in the assembly we said 'goodbye' to Gill Jasper. Gill is retiring from North for the second time. Gill has had a distinguished career serving schools in Colchester. She was a Headteacher for a number of years before deciding she wanted to return to the classroom. Then she came to North and was a brilliant SENCo for a number of years before retiring... for the first time. Deciding that she was missing North too much she returned a year later as a teacher jobshare. Today she retires again. This time I fear it may be permanent as she is moving out of the area. Gill loves North and North loves Gill so I am sure we have not seen the last of her. There is something about this School that people find hard to shake off. In the words of the Eagles, 'You can check out any time you like, but you can never leave.'

And the inaugural winner of the Most Christmassy Classroom was announced. Congratulations to 5NJ.

Classes hold their Christmas Parties in the afternoon. Covid rules observed so no sharing of party food. Whilst the parties are going on I email parents reminding them of the need to inform me over the holiday if their children test positive. The risk of children and staff having to isolate will not pass until Christmas Eve. That is a dark cloud hanging over us all.

Class 5NJ, winners of the Most Christmasy Classroom competition

'No choice but to open our nursery'

Monday, January 18
WEEK three of lockdown. The weekend was spent in communication with the LA – we will have no choice but to offer to open the nursery. What has made the situation worse is the feeling the LA has not been lobbying on behalf of settings only open to their critical worker and vulnerable children. The only help the LA has given settings is, in recognition of the late notice from Government, an extension to the census date from January 21 to January 25. That will give us a couple of extra working days to sort this.

■ Keeping in touch - Toby Gill, one of North Primary School's home learners of the week, speaking to headteacher Alan Garnett

Week Beginning Monday 4th January 2021
(in theory)

Wednesday 30th December 2020

At 4.00pm the wait is over. The noise over what the Government will do about schools in the face of the exponential growth in the transmission rate has become deafening. Gavin Williamson announces in the House of Commons that not all primary schools will open for all their pupils next week. But schools have to wait until the list of areas is published on the Government website. An anxious wait ensues. 5.00pm the list appears and Essex has been split across the middle. The Contingency Framework comes into effect for South and Mid, meaning schools and colleges will be welcoming back children of critical workers and children classed as vulnerable. Colchester, Utttlesford and Tendring primary schools must open as normal.

Thursday 31st December

I send an email to Clare Kershaw.

I am writing to ask you if you are as concerned as I am that primary schools in Colchester are expected to open as normal next week. Nick Hulme, CEO of Colchester and Ipswich Hospitals, is imploring residents to stay indoors. I am pretty sure that Colchester infection rates are higher than in some other areas included in App A of the document that was released yesterday tea-time. So, how can re-opening primary schools in Colchester 'protect the NHS'? If you do agree, are you and Mike Gogarty and ECC proposing to lobby Government about this? Once again, we are all having to respond at very short notice to Government orders...

Friday 1st January 2021

I email all staff and Governors,

I hope that you are well and have had a good break from school.

I thought it might be helpful to keep you in the picture following the Government announcement on Wednesday afternoon. Basically, primary schools in Colchester Borough will open as planned.

For us that means a remote learning day on Monday and all children return to school on Tuesday.

It is the same for Tendring and Uttlesford districts. Primary schools in other parts of Essex will only re-open for key workers' children and the vulnerable like Lockdown 1. [My wife's school is in this category and she spent all Wednesday evening and all day yesterday, leaving home at 7.00am and returning at 6.00pm, notifying parents, giving working parents as much notice as possible, and getting her new bubbles set up!]

I did ask Clare Kershaw why Colchester is not included in this group. I will send an email to all parents tomorrow reminding them of our protocols, also explaining why we will re-open fully - there are likely to be many parents anxious about the return...

Sunday 3rd January

What a day! This morning, Boris Johnson, interviewed live on BBC, informs the nation that it is safe for all children to attend school tomorrow. Lunchtime I get news that the largest teachers' union, NEU, and the largest public sector union, UNISON, have advised their members to submit letters saying that it is not safe for them to work in School if all pupils return. They will work from home and they will work in School if opening is restricted to critical workers' children and the vulnerable. Mid-afternoon, Essex County Council announce that it has asked the Government to place all of Essex under the contingency framework and instructed schools in the North East and West to offer remote learning on Monday, open for those limited numbers on Tuesday, and we must wait to see what the Government decide before we know what to do on Wednesday.

At 2.50pm I send parents the following email,

I would like to provide you with the clearest possible picture I can of what is happening this week.

Clare Kershaw, the Director of Education, has just written to all primary schools in Colchester, Tendring and Uttlesford to instruct them to not open fully tomorrow or Tuesday.

Tomorrow, Essex County Council and Public Health Essex well be meeting with the DfE to request that the above districts fall into the same category as the rest of Essex. If this request is granted then the school will only be open to children of Critical Workers and to the 'vulnerable' for the next fortnight. Remote Learning will continue for the rest of the school. In effect this is the same position as Lockdown 1.

Later today, Clare Kershaw will be sending Headteachers a letter to pass on to parents. I will do this once I have received it.

To summarise:
Monday Remote learning for all

Tuesday School open for critical workers' children and children with EHCPs. Remote Learning to continue for the rest of the school.

If you would like your child to attend school on Tuesday please email the school by 9.00am tomorrow morning. If you are a Critical Worker please state your occupation and confirm that there is no other adult in your household who can look after your child(ren) on that day.

Wednesday Decision awaiting instruction from Essex County Council following their meeting with the DfE.

Finally, a message to working parents. The speculation over the past week and the uncertainty this caused must have been intolerable for you. I have complete sympathy with your situation. I wish these decisions had been made sooner but we are all reacting to a rapidly changing situation, driven by the decision-making timescale of the Government. I will continue to keep you updated as soon as I have been informed of Government and ECC decisions.

What an end to the holiday!

Monday 4th January 2021
At 5.30am I record a radio interview with BBC Essex for their Breakfast Show. I will be too busy to be interviewed live after 8.00am.

Remote Learning has already been posted on our interactive platforms for all pupils.

At 9.00am I hold a Zoom meeting with all staff and two Governor representatives. We re-visit our Covid Risk Assessment and I invite all staff to share their concerns, identify which elements of the risk assessment need to be tightened and what measures need to be put in place to make the School safe enough to open for all pupils on Wednesday - if the Government reject ECC's request.

The meeting was really helpful. Throughout the pandemic I have never sensed such anxiety and, in some cases, fear amongst the staff, as that I felt this morning. Six teachers and six support staff emailed Section 44 letters. (Under the Employment Rights Act 1996, which offers protection to an employee, to refuse to work if they believe there is a 'serious or imminent danger' to their health and safety.) This was a difficult decision for them, causing much soul searching and loss of sleep. Day in day out, these colleagues are totally committed to the children. To inform me that they might not do that from Wednesday was alien to them.

At 11.00am, in the conference call with Clare Kershaw, we are told that the DfE has acknowledged ECC's request and a decision will be made tomorrow. Tomorrow! Unbelievable. Parents and staff need to know what they are preparing for. I ask Clare what ECC will do if the Government order our schools to open for all. A fair question to ask, but not one she was able to answer at that time.

I reflect on the morning staff meeting. It is clear to me that we can tighten our control measures in school but we cannot stop the virus being brought into the School - the transmission rate in the community is too high. Also, if we do have to open in full, I will not be able to open every class anyway because I will not have enough staff. I call my Chair of Governors and we convene an emergency Governors meeting for 5.00pm.

Before the meeting has even started Scotland announces it is going into full lockdown and the PM will be speaking to the country at 8.00pm. The indication is he will announce the same for England. Lockdown.

I explain to the Governors that I do not think it is safe for the School to open fully on Wednesday and I had called the meeting because I did not want to wait any longer for the DfE to make their decision. Parents needed to know. The Governors were in full support but we agreed that I should wait to hear the PM's announcement. I prepare two emails. Which one I send dependent upon the PM's words.

At 8.45pm I emailed parents the following message:

You may have seen the Prime Minister just announce that we must only open to children of critical workers' and to vulnerable children. This does not change our plans for tomorrow. Those parents have been informed of the arrangements. The remainder of the school population will access learning remotely. Staff will make phone calls to those families this week and interactive communication will be maintained through Tapestry or SeeSaw. Free school meals will be available for collection to those eligible who wish to have them. Parents doing the school run: please observe all social distancing rules in and around the school. Let us hope that this and the other measures announced will suppress and reduce the infection rate in the local community as quickly as possible.

The PM did announce that Nurseries should open as normal. I have to say that caught me by surprise and I will explore the possibility for that to happen from Wednesday. I will email our Nursery families tomorrow...

Will we ever know if the DfE was going to agree to ECC's request and whether ECC would have defied the DfE if it had been denied?

Tuesday 5th January

Seven year group bubbles open. Having two teachers per year group helps - one to teach in School, one to manage remote learning. Support staff help in school and will also help making phone calls to parents and children, just like in lockdown 1. Now that parents know this arrangement will continue until Half-Term, I was anticipating a number of new requests for places. There were not many.

I meet with the Nursery teachers who were alarmed by the PM's announcement. They see themselves as part of the school, which they are, and the risks are the same. I send an email to Nursery parents:

I am writing to you, as promised, to tell you what is happening with the Nursery during lockdown. Judging from conversations some of you have had with the Nursery staff, you were as surprised as we were by the announcement Mr. Johnson made last night, that Nurseries can remain fully open. I think many of you were also as shocked as we were too. The reason for limiting numbers in schools is to help to limit the transmission of the virus in the community – and Nursery children and staff count as community too! Therefore, for the safety of the children, staff and families, Nursery children will follow the same rules as the schoolchildren. That is: Remote learning for all children to be accessed via Tapestry, unless parents are critical workers without any other adult in the household to provide childcare, or if the child has an EHC Plan (a statement of additional and complex needs). The teachers will be phoning you this week to explain how the home learning will work...

Following queries from the LA and Unions it has been confirmed by the DfE that school-based Nurseries do have the discretion to open like the rest of their schools.

Day 1 of School lockdown: within a day staff have sorted rotas, got remote learning up and running and set up the Keeping In Touch network with families. A remarkable effort and a great achievement.

Wednesday 6th January

Clare Kershaw sends all schools a letter to forward to parents. I email it with the following message:

Please find attached a letter from Clare Kershaw, Director of Education. You will see that she talks about who could have a place in school, making it clear that it is not an entitlement and with 1 in 50 people in England now infected with Covid the need for as many of us to isolate in our homes and reduce transmission rates and so reduce pressure on our hospitals is ever greater. I will be frank with you, pretty much any working person could make a case that they meet the critical worker category. I exaggerate but you see my point. To offer places to every child meeting the criteria would make a nonsense of the purpose of the lockdown. In applying my duty of care to children and staff in school I am limiting bubble sizes to 12 - one bubble per year group. Thank you to those of you who are making sacrifices, keeping your children at home and juggling home learning and work. It is really appreciated. Teachers are sympathetic to the pressures you face in managing home learning - some have school age children themselves! We are pretty much full in some bubbles so all future requests may be added to our waiting lists...

I spend the afternoon updating the risk assessment for Lockdown 3 and send it to staff for consultation.

Gavin Williamson announces in the House of Commons that exams will not be sat this Summer. He also announces that parents can report schools to Ofsted if they are not happy with their children's remote learning offer. Helpful.

Thursday 7th January

Looking at a Newsletter I sent out on Day 4 of Lockdown 1, back in March last year. It contained advice to parents about managing home learning. I had forgotten how few children attended School in the beginning: 8 on Day 3, 12 on day 4. If we fill all our bubbles, we will have 96 pupils, about 20% of our School population. But the pressure on schools to take more pupils is growing.

The Government announces a U-turn. School-based Nurseries should open in full. That will not help bring the infection rate down. The Local Authority has said that it will support schools' Risk Assessments. My risk assessment says bubbles of 12. I will not be opening the Nursery to all.

Friday 8th January
I email all staff and Governors.

Well, it has been some week! It has been very stressful for all in our community. The Governors have been resolute and they, and we, will have to remain strong over the coming weeks. You will be aware that there is huge pressure on schools to take more and more pupils back; pressure stoked by the DfE's ever-changing guidance. There is also another new directive for our Nursery to open in full. (A U-turn on a U-turn, I make that a 360º!)

I am grateful to one of our parent Governors who has shared the situation working parents face from employers who are now thinking that their employees can work as normal - even if at home - because the children are entitled to places. The media fuel this as well. Last night BBC Look East invited viewers to tell them of schools that denied their child a place.

I must, and will continue to, point out that the guidance still does say that parents should try to keep their children at home. Rightly so. How can we suppress transmission rates if we fill our classrooms?

Following my ParentMail earlier in the week, some parents withdrew their requests, at inconvenience to themselves. I am very grateful to them. Now to home learning. I will be speaking to SMT about this on Monday. As far as I am concerned our approach is the right one. It is interactive and has built in flexibility, acknowledging the juggling acts that all parents perform daily. But, as Gavin Williamson has invited parents to report schools to Ofsted, we will just need to look at our offer and make sure we are compliant.

The year group newsletters I have seen are great (thanks) and I am looking forward to seeing the others - please remember to send them to all staff for reference.

Regarding Keeping In Touch calls. If you have trouble making contact, please check with the teachers of the siblings (if they have any) before informing me...

6.00pm. I relax at home, at the end of an exhausting week. I look through the papers, two stories catch my eye: SAGE scientists say there are too many children in school, the lockdown may have to go on for longer; Ofsted has been inundated with letters from parents - praising the schools for their amazing efforts this week.

Monday 11th January
Week 2 of Lockdown 3. A quiet weekend with no changes announced. Which is a shame regarding our Nursery.

There remains an issue with early years funding. The guidance states that providers will only receive Free Early Education Entitlement (FEEE) funding for children present on census day (on the 21st January), and not for all those on roll, which is how the School is funded. So, children who would attend Nursery but are not because of the pandemic but who are receiving remote learning and pastoral support from the teaching team, will not be counted. This is a huge worry for the sector. If this policy is not changed many private early years settings, still recovering from Lockdown 1, may go under. The maintained sector will be hammered too. Local Authorities and Unions continue to lobby Government to fix this. Let us hope they succeed. This policy will cost our Nursery thousands.

We are notified at 1.30pm that a pupil in Year 4 has tested positive. The pupil only came in on the first day of Term. The bubble are sent home and will have to isolate.

Food has been delivered for the hampers which will be ready to go home tomorrow.

Tuesday 12th January
We have 70 children eligible for Free School Meals: 14 are attending School so get their lunch in School. 23 hampers have been made and will be collected during the morning. These numbers suggest 33 parents have declined the offer which is disappointing. We are offering a weekly food hamper because it was the preferred choice of the Government. We have been happy to go with hampers this time because families need the food now. When we ran the voucher system during Lockdown 1 there were teething problems so families did not get their vouchers for several weeks.

Wednesday 13th January
There is only one story in the news. There are photos of food hampers posted on social media showing a small amount of food, some items lack nutritional value. I do not want our families to think our hampers are like those. And I am trying to get more eligible families to order them. The pictures in the news will not encourage them to apply. I send an email to all families. I explain that our hampers give parents the ingredients to make five substantial lunches for their child(ren). And that if the Government direct us to set up a voucher system again then we will. In the meantime, we will continue to prepare hampers. I also remind parents that for families in extreme need there is also the opportunity to get vouchers for the Colchester Foodbank and the Foodbank also sends home hampers during the School Holidays.

The Government changes its guidance on Free School Meals - they no longer say they prefer schools to provide hampers. A national voucher system will be reintroduced and schools will get information next week. The company managing the scheme is to be the same company that made such a mess getting it up and running last time. So, we will continue to provide hampers whilst we set up the voucher scheme. That way children will not miss out over the next couple of weeks.

This afternoon Gavin Williamson announced that national tests and assessments will not go ahead in primary schools this year, although he did not make a statement about the Foundation Stage Profile - the assessment report for children at the end of their Reception year.

He also said, '*Those early years are so important*,' when speaking to the Education Select Committee to answer why the sector must remain open in full. Well, I wonder if he realises that the impact of the Treasury's position to fund the sector based on attendance on census day rather than number on roll will devastate these settings. We know they are important. Fund us properly.

Thursday 14th January

There were a few responses to my email about Free School Meals. A few more families have ordered them. One asked if the hampers could be delivered as hers was too heavy to carry - so presumably our hampers are substantial. And another parent wanted to donate £100 towards the cost of them - such kindness and generosity.

The LA confirmed its position on lateral flow tests (LFTs), which is the same as many LAs and is at odds with the DfE and DHSC. The LA is saying that staff won't carry out the tests on the pupils and that schools should continue to send bubbles home. The Government policy is as follows: if a LFT is positive the pupil or member of staff is sent home and instructed to get a PCR test (polymerase chain reaction). The rest of the bubble remain in school and have daily LFTs. There are concerns about the high number of false negatives which these tests produce, meaning asymptomatic positive cases would remain undetected and in school. The LA believe that we will not bring down the transmission rate if we follow Government policy. In other words, we should not rely on unreliable tests. Sensible.

The lateral flow test kits will arrive in School on the 18th - these are for staff, not pupils. Training webinars will be online next week as well.

Friday 15th January

The Home Learner of the Week Award has been re-introduced. One child from each year group has been nominated. I will ring them next week to congratulate them.

It is announced that the Foundation Stage Profile will be optional this year.

There has been a change in the Government position on Early Years Funding. It is still a headcount but we can include in the census other children whose parents have made the decision themselves not to send in their children. But for settings that have made the decision that it is not safe to open in full, there will still be a severe financial cost as a LA finance officer writes:

If your decision is to keep the places offered limited to the children of key worker children and vulnerable children you will not be able to access any further funding for the children not attending. If this is the case, and this reduction in funding is unsustainable, you would need to review the financial position of your nursery to decide on your next steps.

This is terrible news. A local Headteacher tells me that she has no choice but to re-open - this is a *'gun to my head'* situation. I am now faced with the same dilemma. If I, and my Nursery staff team, thought it was safe to open for all our Nursery children we would be open. I spend the evening on the phone to the LA expressing my concerns and then record my views in a letter.

Monday 18th January

Week 3 of Lockdown 3. The weekend was spent in communication with the LA - we will have no choice but to offer to open the Nursery. What has made the situation worse is the realisation that the LA has not been lobbying on behalf of settings only open to their critical worker and vulnerable children. The only help the LA has given settings is, in recognition of the late notice from Government, an extension to the census date from the 21st to the 25th January. That will give us a couple of extra working days to sort this.

At the 11.00 meeting with Clare Kershaw, we discuss our email correspondence. She is fully aware of the strength of my feelings and other Headteachers in a similar situation. She offers to write a letter to Heads apologising for not making it clear to that the LA was not actually lobbying Government on behalf of those settings only partially open. In contrast some LAs have instructed their Nurseries not to open and will be funding them in full. Scotland's Nurseries remain closed.

At 12.00 I send an email to Nursery parents:

Firstly, I would like to thank you for your understanding of why the nursery places have only been made available to 'vulnerable' children and children of critical workers, in line with how the rest of the school is operating. However, I have now been instructed by the Local Authority that I must offer to open the Nursery in full. If I do not do this, we will not get funding for this Term and the future of the nursery will be in jeopardy. The Local Authority - under the direction of the Government - has said that we can only claim funding for children with completed Free Early Education Parent/Carer Agreement Forms, as long as the children are either in nursery on headcount day, or their parents have decided that they do not think it is safe for their child to attend during lockdown. Headcount day will be Monday 25th January. I would like your help please in doing the following: 1. The school office will phone any family whose FEEE forms have not yet been returned. These will need to be returned by Friday 22nd January. 2. Please email the school by Thursday 21st January to let us know whether you would like your child to return to Nursery from Monday 25th January or whether, for safety reasons, you would prefer to keep them at home. The staff will continue to post work on Tapestry and keep in contact with you. Over the next couple of days nursery staff will phone you to discuss this situation with you.

The IT technician has started work configuring the laptops for loan. We have received from the Government 26 laptops for '*disadvantaged children who do not have access to a device and whose face-to-face education is disrupted.*' In the first instance these laptops will be offered to our oldest pupils. Parents have been invited to email to request a device.

The afternoon is a lovely distraction spent chatting with the Home Learners of the Week and their proud parents. It was lovely to listen to them talking about their work. Maths activities seem to be the most popular. These children have stood out to their teachers not just because of the amount of work they are doing but how hard they are trying to do the tasks they are finding trickier. The older children are also posting their own comments and questions about their work. The children tell me they are finding ways to keep busy and get fresh air when they are not doing their home learning. What they all miss about not being in School is seeing their friends of course but some are able to keep in touch through online games and/or social media.

I attend the first of two Government webinars explaining the procedures for primary schools to manage the lateral flow testing of staff.

Home learner Toby

3.15 I hold a Zoom meeting with Nursery staff agreeing the plan for the week.

Tuesday 19th January
We can now use the gas ovens in the kitchen. The new extractor hood and all the associated works are complete. Happy Cook.

Hopefully the last food hampers have been put together and collected. The voucher system is being set up to start next week.

Nursery teachers spend the day on the phone to the parents. We have 36 children registered to attend morning, afternoon or all-day sessions. Currently three critical workers' children attend all-day. They are having a lovely time in the Reception bubble.

Wednesday 20th January
In my Governors' meetings this morning I reassure them that we are able to re-open the Nursery safely and not be penalised financially.

Spoke to the Nursery teachers. It is pretty clear now how many parents are wishing to send their children back on Monday. A few are still thinking about it but very few feel comfortable doing this and are writing to confirm that. So, to meet demand and open with due regard to the safety of the children and staff from Monday the Nursery will open a morning bubble of eight and an afternoon bubble of eight. Children who have all-day places will be in the Reception bubble.

In the newsletter I keep all the parent body informed of the situation:

At the beginning of Lockdown, the decision was taken to treat the Nursery the same as the School and open along the same lines. This was within the rules before they were changed. Now the Government is also insisting that Nurseries will only get funding for children who are in attendance or who would but parents have made the decision that it is safer for the children to stay at home and comply with the national effort to suppress the transmission of the virus. Obviously if we thought it was safe to open the Nursery in full, we would have done that already. Over the weekend of the 16th/17th, it was confirmed that if we do not offer to open the Nursery in full, we would not get full funding for this Term for the children registered. Apparently the hours the staff spend providing remote learning, interacting with parents on Tapestry and keeping in touch over the phone do not count. That ruling could mean a loss of funding of up to £30,000, putting the future of the Nursery in jeopardy. This has put all Early Year providers across the country in a terrible position. We have no choice but to offer to open. Meetings have been held with Nursery staff. The teachers spent the 19th and 20th speaking to every family. The School Risk Assessment will be updated.

I pass on a letter to parents from Clare Kershaw and Mike Gogarty, explaining the Essex policy on lateral flow tests. In essence, they write, these tests produce too many false negatives so they will be used by Schools but not in the way the Government intended: Schools should continue to send bubbles home to isolate if somebody tests positive rather than keep them in School and test them every day as per Government policy. Primary schools will get the kits to test staff twice a week from the 25th January.

Obviously these tests will be given to our Nursery staff as well. But the Government will not be issuing kits to Maintained Nursery Schools until February. So the sector that should have been open all the time through lockdown gets their staff test kits last. Shocking.

The kits have been delivered. We have enough tests to last us three months.

Thursday 21st January
Today is census day for Schools and early years settings across the country. This information determines the calculations upon which our budget is set. Obviously we will complete our census on Monday when the Nursery re-opens.

Is it a coincidence that all over the national TV stations today there are reports of the very high number of early years staff who have contracted Covid since December? Very worrying.

Friday 22nd January
The final headcount is in for Nursery. Of the 36, five will be attending all day and there are only six more whose parents would like to return next week ,so at this number we only need to open the morning bubble. This number may grow and

if need to we can open the afternoon bubble. The remaining parents have sent letters to explain their concerns about sending their children into Nursery during lockdown.

Seven parents of Year 6 pupils are informed their requests to borrow a laptop have been granted. They will be available to collect on Tuesday, subject to the signing of a loan agreement. I email Year 5 parents inviting them to request a laptop.

The week finished with a Zoom meeting with all staff to go through the procedures for the self-administering of the lateral flow tests. The recommendation is for all staff working in School to take the test twice every week - before the start and midway. As always, the most useful part of these kinds of briefings is the questions and comments colleagues make. The Government recommendations do not seem best fit when most of our staff are on a fortnightly rota during lockdown: one week in School and one week working from home. So, it is agreed that staff will take an 'exit' test at the end of their week in School. That way staff will know if they are positive and we can take swifter action to notify parents and Public Health and help suppress the spread of the virus.

Monday 25th January

Week 4 of Lockdown 3. Last night staff self-administered lateral flow tests for the first time. Not the most pleasant of activities - swabbing your tonsils and nostrils. All test results have to be reported online to the Government and recorded by the School. No positives.

The Nursery re-opened this morning. Five children attended the morning session. These families are entitled to 15 hours in the Nursery. Five others, entitled to 30 hours, are in the Reception class bubble. The remainder of parents prefer to keep their children at home.

The Food Voucher system was launched without a hitch this time. Eligible families will receive three weeks' worth of vouchers which will take them up to Half-Term.

After School, Senior Leaders meet via Zoom as is usual now. We discuss the findings of the teacher survey. It is clear that more pupils are doing more work than during Lockdown 1. There are a few families who are of concern. Staff have been working hard to make contact and provide advice and support. What is obvious is that the teachers much prefer having all the children in School. We also discuss other ways that we can help families - resource packs will be prepared for collection. I report these findings to the Governors' Curriculum Committee in the evening. The Parent Governors fully appreciate the lengths staff are going to support the children and their parents. One Governor emailed me afterwards - *It's easy to have kind words for exceptionally wonderful, dedicated and caring people.*

Tuesday 26th January

The DfE announce that Schools will be closed during Half-Term but we will be expected to monitor emails and report positive cases to Public Health, as we did over Christmas.

6 Laptops were collected today. This will make a difference. The children will be able to work with greater independence and ease. Parents had to sign a loan agreement. They must obviously take care of it, it must only be used by the child for their school work and it remains the property of the School. A kind and generous grandparent had offered to pay insurance costs for a number of these devices. She had read that this is what needed to have happened. I rang her and thanked her but said that it was not necessary. She will make a donation to the School in another way.

Wednesday 27th January

The day is spent eagerly awaiting a statement from the PM. When will the lockdown measures be eased? At 1.30pm I was listening to a talk online. I felt very sorry for the speaker as he knew his audience were only half-listening to him because they were also listening to Mr. Johnson, addressing the House of Commons.

We now know Schools will not be fully opened before March 8th and that will depend on certain factors. More precise details will be announced on February 22nd - the first day after the Half-Term break. Let the speculation begin.

Thursday 28th January

I send an email to parents to make sure they know the situation. I also remind them of how staff are helping them support home learning -

So, in the meantime, the teachers will continue to teach remotely for the majority of children. I know you and your children appreciate the feedback and comments the staff give - on average, in total, the staff are posting over 1,000 responses a day. That is a remarkable effort – matched by your commitment to home learning whilst juggling all the other balls at home.

There are other ways that the teachers are doing their very best to help you help your children with their home learning. Teachers try to put themselves in your shoes by trying to limit the amount of resources and equipment you would need at home for the children to complete their work. Nevertheless, you will always need some things.

At the start of Lockdown 1, staff prepared resource packs for the children. We are planning to do this again, upon request. Your children's teachers will contact you directly with the list of resources they will include in the packs. You can then let them know if you would like one. You will be able to pick up the packs the first week after Half-Term. This will be timetabled and we will let you know nearer the time the collection times. Look out for the messages from the teachers.

I receive an email from the Chair of the North School Association. A parent has contacted him to say that she made and sold festive wreaths at Christmas and would like to donate the proceeds to the School. Lovely.

Friday 29th January

There has been limited take-up of the laptop loans. Staff make contact with some families. One Dad said they would love a laptop for their son but they felt other families might have a greater need. Another parent, cries in gratitude and relief when she is offered a laptop for her son. Laptops will be collected on Monday.

'Children are working
even harder this time'

Monday 1st February
Week 5 of Lockdown 3. The percentage of children in School hovers around 16%. It was slightly above the national (England) average but that has crept up to the same figure. Infection rates are falling but still higher than in November during Lockdown 2.

There continues to be a lot of talk in the national media about the impact of remote learning on 'disadvantaged' pupils. In other words, the thinking is that the attainment gap is growing. Changes in funding rules will not help this. Up until this year the Pupil Premium Grant (the additional money schools receive, principally based on the number of children on roll who are registered for free school meals, to accelerate the progress of the disadvantaged pupils) was calculated using numbers from the January census. This year the Government is calculating the grant for the Financial Year 2021-2022 taking the numbers from the October census. This will have a negative impact on all schools because during the pandemic the number of families falling into poverty has risen. So at North, our Pupil p#Premium numbers have grown from 79 to 85 between the two census days. PP is funded at £1,345 per pupil, which is £8,000 that we would have received had the rules not changed. Local Authorities and Unions are lobbying the Government's decision. Let us hope they are successful and the Government has a rethink.

A first this afternoon. One of the Home Learners of the Week moved Schools during Lockdown 3 and has never been to North and never met her teacher! How strange must that feel for her. It was lovely to chat with her and her mum.

Tuesday 2nd February
There has been a development in the arrangements for the Year 6 annual residential trip to Osmington Bay, Weymouth. The children should have gone last September but that was rescheduled to this coming April. We are planning for the trip to go ahead whilst waiting for the Government to make an announcement about these types of trips later this month. The more time we have between the present and the actual trip the more likely it is that the trip will be allowed to go ahead. So, at no extra cost to the parents, trip organiser Mrs. Walker has moved the date to as late as possible in the Summer Term. It has not been moved that far back but those few weeks could make all the difference. Let's hope the vaccine programme, the weather and the falling R rate will enable this trip to go ahead. This year, more than ever, our Year 6's need this kind of experience.

Wednesday 3rd February
Yesterday the DfE updated its guidance on Covid-secure measures. Tighter measures for close contacts of symptomatic and positive cases have been introduced. The guidance also makes it clearer that schools decide if a child is classed as 'vulnerable' and not the parent.

Out of the blue I received an email from Alex Bedford, an education consultant who worked with the School. He is about to publish his latest book, Pupil Book Study -

I've written a few words about how I was inspired by the first pupil who took part - Abigail. I wanted to check that it was okay to mention her and dedicate the book to her.

Abigail died two years ago. At her memorial service in School, I played the clip of Alex interviewing Abigail when she was seven. It was a magical interview and I can see why it would have made such an impression on Alex. I email Abigail's parents and they give their permission.

Thursday 4th February
The day begins with top-up training on safer recruitment procedures. I have to do this every three years. I do a home visit in the afternoon and end the day attending a multi-agency Teams Meeting about another family.

Friday 5th February
Sir Kevan Collins has been appointed as the Government's 'education recovery commissioner'. I heard him speak at an Essex Primary Headteachers event a few years ago when he was head of the Education Endowment Fund. He was very impressive. I wonder what his plans will look like and whether he has a view on changes to Pupil Premium funding.

The PM has talked about summer schools. This has not gone down well in my house. My youngest daughter's response is - *'great, the last thing kids want when we get our summer back is to go to school or college!'* I see her point.

Surely we can do better than this kind of catch-up recovery programme for our children. There is so much talk about the damage being done to the children's mental health and yet thinking seems to be limited to rolling out cramming schools. And why do they need to catch up? What is the rush? These children will be working for 50+ years. Let's keep the children in School for an extra year and re-energise the early years' sector. This sector, which the Government is rightly quoted as calling *'vital'* and *'crucial'* has been hammered by Covid and years of underfunding. Let's have a long-term vision for recovery. Invest in the early years, grow the sector and get our four-year-olds to start School a year later. Do that and maybe there will not be such a wide attainment gap when the children start School.

I really hope that Sir Kevan will be given the licence to build a long-term vision and not be restricted to throwing money at a short-term, short-sighted bodge.

Monday 8th February
Week 6 of Lockdown 3.

The return of the Beast from the East. Lovely fresh snow everywhere. When I arrive at School just after 7.00am the Site Manager is busy clearing the front pathway and car park. I tell him to leave the playgrounds – the children will love coming in via Victoria Chase and walking through the snow.

This week is national E-Safety Week. I use my assembly to give guidance to parents and children on the safe use of the internet and social media.

Clare Kershaw confirms that the Government will not budge on their decision to change the funding arrangements for Pupil Premium, which will mean we miss out on £8,000 in the next Financial Year.

Have some lovely conversations with the Home Learners of the Week. Glad to hear they have been playing out in the snow, as their emailed photos for the School newsletter confirm.

Tallulah and Maisie

Tuesday 9th February
It is always worse on day two after heavy snowfall. The snow has been compacted and turned to ice. One teacher could not get her car off the drive, was walking to the bus stop, slipped and has hurt her back. She is unable to come to work today. Send out message instructing parents to enter the School via the front entrance

as Victoria Chase and its pavements are too slippery. Will probably keep these arrangements in place until the snow and ice disappears. When we have reluctantly had to close for snow in the past it has mainly been because the pavements around the School are impassable, not because the staff cannot get to School. The Council do not have the capacity to clear pavements. Have they ever? I think there are some countries where householders have a civic duty to clear the pavement in front of their houses.

Ring the teacher who hurt herself on her journey to work. I am pleased to hear that she is OK, has taken some painkillers and is resting. She confirms she will be back in School tomorrow.

Sir Kevan Collins, whose job title will no doubt be shortened to Recovery Tsar, has made some encouraging statements about Education Recovery. He talks of the impact of lockdown on all the age groups, singling out the youngest as missing out on so many important experiences which will stall their social development - the foundation on which their academic learning is built. This is exactly what we need to hear from the Head of the Commission - looking at the big picture.

The Year 6 bubble has a wonderful time in the garden this afternoon with Wayne Setford from Together We Grow. They built a fire, made hot chocolate and toasted some marshmallows.

Wednesday 10th February
In the media there is growing speculation about re-opening and catch-up programmes. February 22nd is still being billed as the big day for when we will be told about the plans for re-opening Schools which of course have always been open. A colleague Head came across this on Monday from the DfE blog:

The current national measures are driving the R rate down and we hope to be able to start welcoming back more pupils from 8 March at the earliest. It is important to reiterate that we do not see this as a 'return to school' but more of an expansion of the numbers of pupils already in school and receiving a face-to-face education.

Interesting. A very cautious approach.

Much talk of Summer Schools alongside the confused messages about Summer Holidays. If Summer Holidays are back on families will be desperate to get away and I predict a lot will also be booking holidays through the Autumn Term, especially if August is judged as too soon. And many families choose Term-Time holidays because they are much cheaper - even with a non-school attendance fine on top. Will all parents prioritise Summer School and Term-Time School over a family holiday?

Thursday 11th February

Attend a Zoom meeting along with 250 Essex Primary Heads. Clare Kershaw briefs us and holds an extended Q&A. Along with other Local Authorities in the Eastern Region, she met with Government officials yesterday, including the East of England Regional Schools Commissioner, Sue Baldwin. The LAs presented a 'consideration paper' making it clear that there must be clear and compelling evidence for the education roadmap out of Lockdown 3.

Full Governing Body Meeting this evening. They always get the balance right between challenge and support. They are keen to perform their monitoring role effectively but do not want to add unnecessarily to the teachers' burden, conscious as they are of how hard teachers and the support staff are working at the moment. Long discussions are held about Autumn Term attainment and attendance data and the welfare of children during Lockdown 3. It is clear that the youngest pupils' progress has been affected the most. KS1 and KS2 pupils in total missed 819 days in school in the Autumn Term for Covid-related reasons, which works out on average at just under 2.5 days per pupil.

Friday 12th February

In the certificate assembly this morning I explain to the children that we are exactly half-way through the Academic Year. This moment normally signifies surviving Winter and the prospect ahead of trips, tests and lots of events.

Last night the Parent Governors agreed to hold a meeting in the near future to share their perceptions of remote learning so that they can get an overview across all age groups. To help them I email all this week's teacher newsletters. These letters really are amazing. The Governors will see consistency. They are clear and informative and, most importantly, they will also see that the tone is perfect - one of celebration, support and encouragement.

Email the parents of children in School to remind them that they must inform the School if their children test positive during the holiday. If any children (and staff) who are symptomatic over the weekend go on to test positive then I will have to inform the Essex Track and Trace Team and their bubble will have to isolate.

Stand at the School gate and say goodbye to all the children and their parents. Everybody deserves a break from School and from home learning - children, parents and staff.

Ricky in the snow

Saturday 20th February

It has been a quiet Half-Term break. School fire alarm system checked, water supply, legionella checks completed, one child protection conference. Only one family reported positive Covid cases and that was at the end of the week so there was no need to inform parents and staff of a need to isolate. My thoughts turn to the Prime Minister's announcement due on the 22nd. I email staff and Governors.

Good Morning Colleagues,

Not the most exciting of holiday breaks - never have kitchen cupboards been so tidy! But I do hope you have been able to relax and recharge your batteries. It is hard to switch off when the speculation grows daily about what will be announced on Monday. I am conscious that this email will not help you remain switched off but I think you will find it helpful to know how I plan to tackle next week in response to the Government's pending announcements.

Monday 3.30pm PM makes an announcement in the House of Commons.
5.00pm PM TV press conference.

Tuesday DfE plan to publish guidance to provide the detail beneath the PMs headlines.
3.45pm Senior Management Team meeting.

Wednesday NEU national executive to meet. [I do not know about other unions.]

Thursday 11.00 Mike Gogarty joins the conference call with Clare Kershaw and other unions, which I attend.
4.00pm School Change Team Meeting - all invited.

You will be aware that leaks indicate primaries will open in full on March 8th and unions have issued a joint statement urging a more cautious approach.

You may also have read reports that the infection rate amongst younger children is rising - unexpected and alarming news. However, last Thursday I was briefed on Essex data that differs from this national picture that I am sure you will find more reassuring -

Using Feb 8th-12th data Clare Kershaw confirmed that the Eastern Region bucks the national trend and Essex more so. So latest Essex figures for positive cases are as follows -
23-39 years   152
11-18   62
0-10   48
In other words, infection rates amongst our pupil age group is not high and these numbers are coming down. I look forward to seeing half of you on Monday. Enjoy the warmer weather this weekend.

Those Essex figures are very encouraging.

Monday 22nd February
Week 8 of Lockdown 3.

School re-opens with a few more children added to the bubbles.

Steady trickle through the morning of parents who have pre-ordered their free home learning resource packs which will hopefully see them through lockdown.

At 3.30pm in the House of Commons the PM announces the *'roadmap'* out of lockdown, confirming that all Schools in England will open fully on March 8th. He uses the words *'cautious'* and *'irreversible'*, and the phrase *'data not dates'* is used repeatedly. The promise of two weeks' notice has been kept. It seems that there is nothing significantly different for primaries but secondaries will have the logistical challenge of administering three lateral flow tests for all their students, who must also wear masks in lessons. Their return will have to be phased.

Unexpectedly, the DfE has published its guidance during office hours on the same day as the PM's announcement, one day ahead of schedule. This is the first time I can recall over the past year that Government information has come out in a timely fashion. It is a lovely feeling.

Tuesday 23rd February
Send an email to the parents.

I am sure you are keen to know our plans for March 8th. We will be looking forward to welcoming all the children back on that date. The Government has updated its guidance and we are currently working through their main 64-page document and other associated guidance papers. We will be reviewing our school organisation plans accordingly. I will share those plans with you on Friday.

Document read, along with its various links. Basically School will look much like it did in the Autumn with class bubbles, staggered start, break and end of the day times; eating lunch in classrooms and segregated playground zones. This time the clinically extremely vulnerable (CEV) are not allowed to be in School before March 31st, even if they want to, which may well present Schools with staffing issues. We have five staff in that category. Protocols for positive cases will remain the same: send the bubble home for 10 days. The only real issue I have with the document is about After School Clubs: these can start up again and bubbles can be mixed, which seems nonsensical. What is the point of going to extraordinary lengths during the day to limit contact between pupils if they are then allowed to mix on a football pitch or classroom? The guidance makes it clear that student lateral flow testing and the wearing of face coverings in secondary schools will be voluntary. That is problematic.

After School meet with the senior leaders. General feeling of positivity about March 8th, although we do wonder why the four Home Nations continue to follow different paths. We discuss operational matters including organising cover for the CEV staff. We will be contacting families with children who have not been attending because a household member is CEV in the hope that vaccines have been administered and parents will feel confident enough to send their children back to School.

Wednesday 24th February

Gavin Williamson spends the day making announcements about 'catch-up' plans: money for Summer Schools and Tutoring Programmes. It is so frustrating that so much money will be spent on such short-sighted and unambitious plans; plans that will target some pupils but not all. All children and young people have had a year of their education - pre-school, primary, secondary or tertiary - disrupted in the pandemic. Shouldn't the plan be universal?

Thursday 25th February

The meeting with Mike Gogarty is really interesting. *'We are not out of the woods yet,'* is his clear message. Everybody must continue to follow all the rules, he says, he supports the Schools reopening in full as there is a natural circuit breaker in the Easter Holiday. I understand that but that does make it sound like an experiment. What if infection rates start to rise again? I presume the Schools will continue to remain fully open (irreversible) but next steps out of lockdown (March 29th and April 12th) will be put on hold (data not dates).

Very different atmosphere when all the staff meet via Zoom after School. When we met on January 4th there was high anxiety. Today, the mood was positive with full focus on operational matters. Clearly, the biggest job will be to manage parent and children expectations: we are still in lockdown and infection rates are still high.

Friday 26th February

Spend the day updating the risk assessment in the light of the School Change team Meeting, writing a to-do list for issues that need to be addressed before March 8th and writing four emails to parents which I ping out through the day.

10.00am
I am writing to you today as promised. All staff held a Zoom meeting after school yesterday, with Governors in attendance, and plans have been finalised for the full re-opening of the school on Monday March 8th. We are looking forward to welcoming all the children back and meeting the few new arrivals who are now on roll but not been able to attend yet! I will be sending out more ParentMails with the details on getting ready for that event. Please look out for those. In the meantime I will leave you with this message from Mike Gogarty, Head of Public Health Essex, who said yesterday, 'We are not out of the woods

yet.' He is happy for primary schools to re-open in full but reminds us all that we are still in lockdown and we, as a nation, are still a long way from beating Covid and life returning to normal. With that in mind, school will look very similar to what it looked like last term. Look out for further ParentMails.

12.00pm
Please remember only schools are coming out of lockdown. The rules for adults outside the home remain the same – no gatherings, essential journeys only. The school run carries the greatest potential risk to the spread of Covid. Travelling to school - waiting in Victoria Chase, mingling in the playground, waiting in John Harper Street. The one-way system will remain in place for the school children. Please social distance. Only one adult per family on site. Follow a 'grab and go' policy - do not loiter in John Harper St or on the Astroturf (unless you are waiting for another child). I would advise wearing a mask outside of school on the school run too. Please remember everything your child needs before setting off - to avoid unnecessary journeys to the school office with packed lunches and musical instruments. Thank you. Bottlenecks occurred around 8.40 and 3.10 so the staggered start times have been reviewed. They will remain the same for all age groups except Year 5. Year 5 will start at 8.30am and finish at 3.00pm. You will be reminded of these times. We will be introducing waiting zones on the playground and Astroturf to make it clearer where children can be left in the mornings and to ensure that bubbles do not mix. This will be clearly marked. Finally, there is the additional risk of harm to pedestrians - i.e. your children - with cars using Victoria Chase and John Harper Street and parking illegally. Please act responsibly and within the law. Thank you.

1.00pm
I think it is important to remind you of the protocols when there is a positive case. Basically they are the same. So, please do not send your child to school if they are symptomatic. Isolate the household and get them tested. Inform the school of the test outcome and if it is negative the child (and siblings of course) can return to school. If positive, inform the school. Then it will be 10 days isolation for your household and 10 days isolation for the children and staff in that infected person's bubble. The rest of those households do not need to isolate. I will try to make the next email a bit more cheerful.

2.00pm
Dear Parents and Carers, please share this message with your children

Dear Children.

Get the school uniform out - check it still fits - and get ready for the 8th. The arrangements for coats and bags and clothes will be the same as before. Children, make sure you only bring what you need to school - do not forget your water bottle, lunchbox and musical instruments (on the right day!). Bags and coats will be left in the same place as before to avoid crowding in cloakrooms. The teachers will remind you of when PE day is so that you come to school in the correct clothes. We also have two special days coming up. Monday 15th March. Come to school dressed as your favourite book character. Next week is World

Book Day but we will not all be together for that. The teachers will be doing lots of work on favourite books before the 15th which will also help your parents with costume ideas if they need them. Friday 26th March. Easter Parade. Now, we can't all squeeze into the hall as assemblies will still take place via Zoom but that should not stop you making and wearing to school your magical millinery masterpieces (translation: Easter bonnets and hats). So, get creative. I am sure the NSA will think of something to reward all those that take part. Looking forward to seeing you all on the 8th.

Year 6 in the playground

'We're busy getting set to open again'

Monday 1st March

Week 9 of Lockdown 3. The final week of limited school attendance. Let us hope there will be no Lockdown 4.

In assembly I talk to the children about why we study Religious Education (RE) in school. I talk about how RE is a great subject because it helps us to understand ourselves better as we learn about and from others. I talk about how we can learn from the deeds of famous people like Captain Sir Tom Moore and Malala Yousafzai. How their life stories help us think about hope, kindness, courage, charity, selflessness. How RE helps us to understand and celebrate difference. Powerful messages. And I tell them that learning right from wrong, making good choices, showing respect for yourself and others helps us to be the best we can be. At North there are 28 languages, 14 religions and one community. I am looking forward to having all children back as one next week.

The consultation period for staff to respond to the revised Risk Assessment has closed and is now on the School website. In truth it does not vary significantly from the December version. No surprises in the phone calls this afternoon to Home Learners of the Week: the children are looking forward to seeing their friends again. One child thanks me for the laptop loan which he said made all the difference.

The Year 6's who are in school are very happy - well, nearly all of them. They found out which secondary school place they have been offered. Nearly all got the school they wanted.

Tuesday 2nd March

The biggest challenge ahead of next Monday is staffing. We have a number of staff who are not able to work in School for the next few weeks. Even though a few of these colleagues have had vaccines and want to return to School, the guidance does not permit it. Plugging the gaps is top of my to-do list for the rest of the week.

Wednesday 3rd March

Budget Day. No obvious pronouncements on education from The Chancellor. I have a meeting with the School Finance Officer on Friday, to set our own budget, a task that never gets easier.

I pass on a letter from Essex County Council to our parents informing them that they can order their own home testing kits – for them, not their children – directly from the Government.

Finish the day attending a Local Authority run webinar. Essex has an ambitious plan to address the massive national challenge of overcoming the impact of disadvantage on children's education. There is much to commend in the approach. Ring fenced money to 'close the gap' has been in the system for a decade. This 'pupil premium' was and is an excellent initiative but sadly the main gap this money has closed is the gap between what Schools need to spend and what they have to spend, with the well-documented year-on-year under-funding during this same period. And that is not just underfunding in education but also in other public services which support children and their families - pre-schools, social care, mental health and so on. Overcoming these barriers has been made even harder for schools, families and children because of the pandemic. It is right that Essex prioritises disadvantage.

Thursday 4th March
Quiet day. Preparations continue.

Friday 5th March
Budget setting meeting is predictable. Rising costs and the financial impact of Covid means that there is no room for growth. We look at ways of balancing the budget so that we can continue to make the same educational offer as before. It will be tight but at least this year we will not be facing a redundancy situation. Small mercies.

There is an End-of-Term feeling today. Children in School are finishing off and classrooms are being prepared for the return of all the children on Monday. Families are celebrating the end of home schooling today.

Photos and messages have been posted on the learning platforms. Jude, pictured with his sister, Faye, holding all their home learning on their heads, said, '*My mum said, it's a wrap, home school is now closed!*'

Here is another message which I hope sums up how parents across the country feel. '*Hey Teachers, I just wanted to say a HUGE thank you for all the support that we have received during the last however many weeks it has been. SeeSaw has been brilliant; the marking of work has been super speedy and the home calls have been great for continuity. I am sure you have all been tested to your limits juggling the children coming into the school and the ones at home but I think you have done an AMAZING job. I am so glad that my son is at North right now and even more glad that you are all his Teachers. Big socially distanced pats on the back to all of you.*' One parent even went as far as to say that our early years teachers got so good at their video making that they should consider a career on CBeebies!

Thank you all so much for the amazing videos, resources, stories and advice. You have made the challenges pretty pain free and enjoyable for all of us! I would love to see you all do a CBeebies take over one day!

Staffing sorted. The team have pulled together, as always, to plug those staff gaps. Ready for Monday.

Jude and Faye - the end of home learning

Monday 8th March

Week 10 of Lockdown 3 and day 1 of the full re-opening. Well, it was lovely to see so many happy smiley faces at the gate this morning. The children looked happy too! The parents were very pleased to be bringing the children back to School. There is the relief of not being cooped up and the reality for many that they have not been able to work. '*I will be able to earn some money again,*' said one mum. Let us hope that infection rates do not spike and step 1 out of lockdown is a success.

Skipping in the playground

There is no inevitability of success as demonstrated by the Government's publication of an updated Contingency Framework today. This document sets out what would happen if infection rates spike in an area and there has to be a local response. Infants would get priority over juniors for school places if it was a partial opening.

Secondaries are phasing their full return as they are administering the testing of all (voluntary) their students. The take up rate in Essex is about 70%.

After School I met with the Senior Leaders and reviewed the operational arrangements. Staff are happy and the children have had a great day. They will all be tired tonight.

Tuesday 9th March

Receive an email from a friend who lives round the corner. *'Have you set a new fitness regime at school? So many parents and children seemed to be running to North this morning!'* Perhaps the children struggled to get up on day 2. Good to know they are keen to be punctual.

All schools received a letter from Gavin Williamson today singing the praises of staff. Here is a quote:

Leaders, teachers, support staff and all those who are essential to the running of schools and colleges have worked tirelessly to provide both face-to-face provision for vulnerable children and the children of critical workers, alongside remote education for those who have had to stay at home.

For once I am able to agree with him. Not sure that his letter will tip the scales back in his favour with the teachers. An ITV poll in January revealed that 92% thought he should resign. Oh dear.

In conversation with Laura Davison, the CXXV history Project Co-ordinator. We finalise the arrangements for the book launch on the 15th. Her press release includes these words from the project Historian, Claire Driver -

CXXV has been a very special project. We've reached people whose connection with the school stretches back over 100 years enabling us to tell the story from the very beginning. Researching, sharing and celebrating this history with today's pupils and more widely with the people of Colchester has been a real pleasure.'

Claire did a brilliant job. And last year's Year 6's learnt so much about how to be an historian from her. They will all get their own signed copy of the book.

Wednesday 10th March

Busy day for Governors. Finance and Premises Committees met back-to-back. Draft 1 of the budget is close to being balanced. A few savings will need to be made. Premises Committee are told they will have to prioritise their priorities as we may not be able to afford every project in the coming financial year.

There is no need to include a pay award for teachers in the budget as the Government announced a public sector pay freeze last December. Perhaps teachers will feel the nice letter from the Secretary of State is reward enough.

In the evening Parent Governors met to review the lockdown experience. I am sent their minutes at 11.45pm. That is dedication. The two pages were incredibly detailed and showed they had considered every aspect of the experience from the child, the parent and the staff's point of view. The minutes concluded,

It was wholeheartedly and emphatically agreed by all Parent Governors, that all Staff at the School have done an amazingly great job over the past twelve months, in extremely challenging (and at times, difficult and unpredictable) circumstances, and it was further agreed that a letter of appreciation and acknowledgment of their hard work and unwavering dedication is to be drafted and presented to the School.

Thursday 11th March
I was informed today by the Director of Education that the most up to date figures show the infection rate is 70 per 100,000 in Essex. This number is low and falling which is encouraging. So far there are seven Essex secondary school students reporting positive lateral flow test results. Let us hope the figures next week continue to go in the right direction.

Friday 12th March
School attendance this week is just over 97% - in line with the average for Essex primary schools. It is confirmed today that children entitled to Free School Meals will get food vouchers over the Easter Holidays. Good news to end a good week.

Eating in the classroom.

Monday 15th March
Week 11 of Lockdown 3 and week two of the full re-opening.

Theo and Auden Dagge. Their grandmother, Jenny Keeble, taught in the Nursery for 40 years. They found her photograph in the book.

Children came to School dressed as their favourite book characters to celebrate World Book Day. I know it was actually on March 4th but most of the children were not in School so we wanted to hold it when everybody could take part. The children and staff looked amazing. They all had a wonderful surprise in assembly. They were joined via Zoom by Laura Davison and Claire Driver, to announce the publication of a brand-new book. CXXV - the history of our School. Laura and Claire, Project Co-ordinator and Historian respectively, are the authors. They were thanked for their amazing achievement. It was pointed out to the children that it is not usual for a School to have a book written about itself. And what makes this book extra special is that the children - especially the year group who are now in Year 7– helped to make it: the children learnt how to be real historians, finding out about the past at first hand, creating an archive to go alongside the book. We are grateful to the National Lottery Heritage Fund who provided the funds to make the whole project possible. Every family will receive a copy, as will staff and Governors. Year 7's will also get their own personal copy.

The book will now be on sale online via the www.northschoolcxxv.com website. When shops re-open fully Red Lion Books in Colchester and Firstsite will stock copies. BBC Essex will tomorrow at 4.00pm be interviewing Laura, Claire and former pupil Jessica Dines, last years Chair of the School Council. Who knows, perhaps TV will be next.

The 15th March will go down as another remarkable day in the remarkable history of North Primary School and Nursery.

Claire Driver, CXXV Historian, left. Image: Adrain Rushton.

Laura Davison, CXXV Project Co-ordinator, right.

Tuesday 16th March

Lovely atmosphere at the School gate this morning. The youngest children were excited to tell me they had seen my photo in the book and the parents were very complimentary of the book, recognising what an amazing achievement it is.

I was encouraged by the words of the new Children's Commissioner, Dame Rachel de Souza. Her first media appearance in role gave the right message - the education recovery plan should involve children and young people, she said - she is calling it *The Big Ask*. I could not agree more. (I have an article due to be published in Schools Week making that same point.)

BBC Essex has postponed the live radio interview this afternoon. Apparently singer Joss Stone is going to steal our slot. An outrage. The interview will now take place next Monday.

The rest of the day was more sombre, spent in conversation with social workers and other safeguarding professionals. They tell me that their case-load has risen exponentially since all the children have returned to School.

Wednesday 17th March

The Blackwater Partnership is a group of schools co-ordinated from Thurstable, a secondary school in Tiptree. It organises a huge calendar of sporting events for primary and secondaries. Inter-school sports are obviously not happening but the partnership has been creative, organising in-school and remote learning activities. Certificates were presented in assembly to children who have demonstrated good team work, passion and determination. There was also a certificate for the School - children could take part in a walking challenge and collectively they walked 93 miles.

Ofsted announced today that full inspections would not resume before the start of the Autumn Term. That is one less distraction schools will have to worry about. There will still be inspections in the Summer Term. What these will look like is currently being piloted.

The School budget is balanced. Savings have been made across the board including premises. Managing a largely Victorian Grade II Listed Building is not cheap and deferring works will lead to additional costs in the future. These are the difficult decisions all schools face. Missing out on £8,000 to provide bespoke support for disadvantaged pupils due to the Government's 'improvement' to the accountancy procedures is unhelpful. It is widely reported in the newspapers today that this policy change has deprived schools across England of £180 million in the coming financial year.

Thursday 18th March
This afternoon I attended a Zoom meeting of the NAHT branch secretaries of the East of England. We were joined by our new Regional Schools Commissioner who shared with us Ofsted's work in the East over the past Term.

She told us that the Ofsted received 1,500 letters of praise from parents following Gavin Williamson's suggestion that they submit complaints if they are unhappy with schools' remote learning offers. Ofsted responded to everyone. They also received 90 complaints which Inspectors dealt with. Of the 90 just three led to any follow-up action.

Inspections this Term in the East of England have found that schools are taking effective action, are well prepared to deliver remote learning and leaders are basically doing their job and doing it very well. As you would expect but it is still good to hear.

Friday 19th March
Joined 300 Essex primary heads attending our annual conference - remotely of course. The highlight was listening to Mary Myatt, an educational consultant, who spoke so much good sense. She spoke with eloquence and passion about the need to give children the very best resources to lift their learning. She shared an uncomfortable truth - schools spend a fortune photocopying paper to stick in children's exercise books and call themselves eco-schools. Invest in high quality books she said. A perfect message to end our book week.

The first time I have felt the benefit of age - I pop up to the Colchester United Football Stadium to get my first vaccine jab. It is very well organised. A highly efficient operation.

Get home, catch up with the news. France and Poland entering their third waves. New lockdowns imposed. Not a good sign.

Monday 22nd March

Week 12 of Lockdown 3, week three of the full re-opening and the final week of the Spring Term. And a whole year since all the pupils at North were first denied their right to attend School.

In assembly this morning I gave the children the opportunity to reflect on the pandemic. Using photos, I reminded the children of how School life had changed over the course of the past year. It was an opportunity to reflect on bravery and loss and individual acts of kindness and thoughtfulness from children, parents and staff. It showed our community at its best.

The morning conference call was also spent in reflection which quickly turned to consideration of the path forward. The LA is establishing an Education Recovery Task Force, the Unions each have their own visions for recovery. There was agreement that the LA's inclusive model of leadership which has evolved over the past year should continue.

Everything stopped at 4.00pm. We all tuned in to BBC Essex. Laura, Claire and Jessica were ready to promote CXXV. No visit to the recording studio in Chelmsford of course. Each sat in their kitchens with their mobile phones, managing their nerves on their own. They did brilliantly. BBC Essex also played a recording of our oldest living former pupil - Margaret Gilbert. Now 106 - born on Christmas Day in 1914. When Margaret was a sprightly 104, she was interviewed in her home by Jacob and Gaby, now both at secondary school. It was lovely to hear Margaret's voice again.

Tuesday 23rd March

How can we make the Summer Term special for our Year 6's in what will be their final Term in primary school? Their residential trip is looking unlikely but we still await the decision from the DfE. After school clubs will resume and the Year 6's will be prioritised. One boy said to me, 'Thank you for letting us play football next term Mr. Garnett.'

Wednesday 24th March

In Good Work Assembly this morning one of the Year 6 classes shared their beautiful words and pictures. They had been looking back on the past year and then thought about their hopes for the coming months. They had produced stunning art work - Trees of Hope, using not just Klimt's painting as inspiration but also Kandinsky's circles which became flowers on the trees. And the children shared their personal hopes. Leah's simple wishes captured the mood perfectly. They finished their presentation by saying, 'Your hopes might be blossoming, just like ours.'

I hope that soon enough I will be able to go on family outings again because I don't get to see them much and I miss my cousins. I also hope that I can start having sleepovers with my friends since I miss watching films and joking about something silly.
Leah

Letter of Hope by Leah, Year 6

Thursday 25th March
A Year 3 class wore their favourite party clothes to School today. They missed the end of the Autumn Term because children and staff were isolating so their class Christmas Party was postponed. They have been looking forward to it all Term.

Friday 26th March
The final day of the Spring Term. Governors Awards presented and the Easter Parade. Normally the 440 children are squeezed into the hall and classes take it in turns to parade in their Easter bonnets. It is a magical sight. No squeezing and no catwalk this year but the children were still excited to be showing off their bonnets in their classrooms. At the end of the day every child left school holding eggs gifted by the North School Association. This year the School will be closed over Easter.

Sitting at home with a glass of wine, looking back on the past 12 months. The School is in its 127th year. It has experienced two World Wars, a General Strike, a three-day week and entering the EEC and leaving the EU. Two Queens, four Kings and eight headteachers! This past year has been extraordinary. How an organisation manages a crisis is a test of its strength and character. North Primary School and Nursery has survived; in fact, in many ways, it has thrived. Paradoxically separation has brought us closer together. And that is due to the remarkable efforts of remarkable people - staff, Governors, parents and the children. Let us hope the coming year is just ordinary.

Tree of Hope by Sophia, Year 6

What next?

Catch-up? It's All Ambition and No Imagination

This "opinion piece" appeared in Schools Week on March 2021. With thanks to the brilliant editing skills of J-L Dutaut.

The greatest shake up in Education since 1944. '*Transformative*,' promises the Secretary of State. There is the ambition, but where is the imagination? Extended schooldays, cramming tutorials, summer schools, a 5-term year...

That's the rescue package? It sounds more like punishment. As my daughter remarked, '*Great, the last thing we want when we get our summer back is to go to school!*' And she's a 16-year-old with a remarkable work ethic. She is desperate to get into her sixth form classrooms and common room.

How quickly the '*recovery plan*' morphed into a '*catch-up programme*'. Who will catch up exactly? To what or to whom? By when? And what is the rush? Exams at 16? Wasn't a major rethink of these long overdue even before Covid?

I am heartened by '*education recovery tsar*' Sir Kevan Collins' comments so far, in particular on what infants have missed. But unless his approach is to stimulate a great debate, I fear the solutions won't be equal to the problems.

The Government's slogan is '*build back better*'. But thinking only about what the children have missed - and in a narrow curricular sense at that - will not deliver that. Take the Early Years sector, for example. Ministers are on record as saying it is '*vital*', yet seem to be in complete denial that it has been devastated by lockdown and successive years of underfunding. The foundations of a recovery plan must be laid there.

There is an obvious solution. It's talked about everywhere in hushed tones like some dangerously radical idea, and it is anything but. But time is running out, so let me be the one to put it out there:

Defer the start of the September 2021 cohort. From today, that would give us five months to rejuvenate and expand the Early Years sector. Our three and four-year-olds would start school a year later, in September 2022. It would give them the time to re-establish pre-school routines, bring us in line with other high-performing nations and create jobs too!

Our current Reception cohort, who missed six months of pre-school and a big chunk of Receptions, will be able to complete it from now and through next year. With the extra time, they won't just catch up but finish ahead! And with more time for those crucial personal and social experiences that are the building blocks for their future learning to boot.

The rest of the primary sector could also complete their year over the course of the next four-and-a-bit terms. At no additional cost to the taxpayer - they are supposed to be in school - teachers will have time to deliver a rich curriculum in depth. This primary phase of a universal recovery plan even has the potential to tackle educational disadvantage before children start school.

At the other end, not all year 10s or 11s may be overjoyed at the prospect of an extra year. But have we asked them? Most may actually favour the chance to sit fair exams, and we would have time to reform them in the meantime.

They have to stay in full-time education or its equivalent until the age of 18 anyway, so let's ask them what they want. The EEF tells us feedback as a low-cost too with a high effect size. Why should that only be the case for classroom practice? They deserve a reward for their forbearance and sacrifices over the past year. Tutoring, weekend lessons and holiday cramming clubs are not that.

If 'recovery' means nothing more ambitious than catch-up then we will make that lazy label, 'the lost generation' a self-fulfilling prophecy. We can and must do better. Every cohort has missed out, so every recovery plan must be universal. And it won't do for 'recovery' to mean recovering a system we intend to reform in the coming years anyway.

A big debate may seem impossible. The timeline only makes it appear more so. But as Nelson Mandela said, 'it always seems impossible until it's done'. If Sir Kevan's appointment is to mean anything, it should be the start of some real political ambition.

Acknowledgements

Over the past year every member of every school community has faced any number of personal and professional challenges. Myself included.

I would like to thank my family and friends for their love and support.

I would also like to thank all my colleagues and Governors for their indefatigable commitment to do the best for the children and their families.

Thank you also to the Colchester Daily Gazette and Newsquest Essex for allowing the use of their photographs and articles.

The newspaper articles have been collated by Sir Bob Russell and will be added to the North School Archive for posterity.

Glossary

ADPH	Association of Directors of Public Health
CEV	Clinically extremely vulnerable
DfE	Department for Education
DHSC	Department of Health and Social Care
ECC	Essex County Council
EEC	European Economic Community
EEF	Education Endowment Foundation
EHCP	Education and Health Care Plan
EU	European Union
FEEE	Free Early Education Entitlement
FSM	Free School Meals
GCSE	General Certificate of Secondary Education
HMI	Her Majesty's Inspector of Schools
HSE	Health and Safety Executive
INSET	In-Service Training Day
KIT	Keeping in Touch phone calls
KS1	Key Stage 1, infant pupils aged between 5 and 7 years old
KS2	Key Stage 2, junior pupils aged between 7 and 11 years old
LA	Local Authority
LSA	Learning Support Assistant
LFT	Lateral Flow Tests
MDAs	Midday Assistants
NAHT	National Association of Headteachers
NSA	North School Association - the School's parents and staff fundraising group
PCSO	Police Community Support Officer
PCR	A polymerase chain reaction test for Covid-19
PHE	Public Health England
PPE	Personal Protective Equipment
SAGE	Scientific Advisory Group for Emergencies
SATs	Standard Assessment Tests
SMT	Senior Management Team
SeeSaw	Interactive learning platform used for home schooling
SENCo	Special Educational Needs Co-ordiantor
SEP	Standards and Excellence Partner - the direct link between the LA and the school
Tapestry	Interactive learning platform used for home schooling